"If you thought he was dangerous on campus, just wait until you meet him in Church."

—Monica Crowley, columnist and
New York Times bestselling author

"A blunt, funny, searing, and accurate depiction of the failed papacy of Francis."

—Leon J. Podles, author of
Sacrilege: Sexual Abuse in the Catholic Church

"Milo's readers won't be scandalized by his devilish attacks on identity politics and its victim tropes. These are signatures of his comedic and literary wit. But like me they may be surprised to learn that his disdain for leftist materialism is based on faith in God and love for His (un)holy Church. In *Diabolical*, Milo turns his wrath on the social justice infiltrators of the Catholic leadership, and especially on the chief culprit among them, Pope Francis, the Pretender. Incendiary."

—Michael Rectenwald,
New York University

"We've seen Milo the troll, the stand-up com dian, the political operative and the dresser. This is Milo the scholar a It's his best incarnation yet."

"He might prove almost as dangerous as he wants us to think he is."

—*Vox.com*

"I stopped believing in God years ago. Milo's book has me questioning my lack of faith, because it proves the Devil exists."

—Mike Cernovich

"A powerful testament from a courageous warrior, whom the left has done everything it can to silence—and failed."

—David Horowitz

"There is no little irony in a gay icon calling out the Vicar of Christ for the wickedness of the Church. But as it is written, the Lord works in mysterious ways."

—Vox Day

DIABOLICAL

DIABOLICAL

HOW POPE FRANCIS HAS BETRAYED CLERICAL ABUSE VICTIMS LIKE ME—AND WHY HE HAS TO GO

MILO YIANNOPOULOS

A BOMBARDIER BOOKS BOOK

ISBN: 978-1-64293-163-1
ISBN (eBook): 978-1-64293-164-8

Diabolical:
How Pope Francis Has Betrayed Clerical Abuse Victims
Like Me—and Why He Has To Go

Cover Design by Milo Yiannopoulos
Photography by Mike Allen

BOMBARDIER
BOOKS

Bombardier Books
New York • Nashville

Published in the United States of America

This book, like all my books, is for my husband, John, who has promised not to read Chapter Two.

Is the Church not simply the continuation of God's deliberate plunge into human wretchedness; is she not simply the continuation of Jesus' habit of sitting at the table with sinners, of his mingling with the misery of sin to the point where he actually seems to sink under its weight? Is there not revealed in the unholy holiness of the Church, as opposed to man's expectation of purity, God's true holiness, which is love, love that does not keep its distance in a sort of aristocratic, untouchable purity but mixes with the dirt of the world, in order thus to overcome it? Can, therefore, the holiness of the Church be anything else but the bearing with one another that comes, of course, from the fact that all of us are borne up by Christ?

—Joseph Ratzinger,
Introduction to Christianity

CONTENTS

FOREWORD

I am a Catholic in part because Milo Yiannopoulos encouraged me towards Rome. I know that will surprise a lot of readers, but it's true. From the moment I became aware of him causing a ruckus on American college campuses, I saw in Milo a depth and seriousness he only hints at in his mischievous and provocative lectures.

Milo's talks got attention because his fearlessness and flamboyance were new to conservative politics. But examine the contents of his talks, beneath the pyrotechnics, and you find a surprisingly orthodox set of commitments—to beauty, to masculinity, to the life of the unborn, and to God. No wonder the Left finds him so confounding and dangerous.

None of his critics on the Right acknowledge that at the heart of Milo's pranks and provocations has always been his fidelity to beauty, universal truth, justice, and his faith. But without those things he could not have written this book. At its heart lies a profound sadness at the corruption of the Catholic Church, an institution which no longer prizes the heroic manly virtues that Milo encourages his student audiences to embrace, and which, he explains, the priesthood must rediscover.

I started life as a Presbyterian, so I was used to seeing female clergy. But I was drawn later in life to a Church with only male priests. I've been meditating on what it means to have a male priesthood that some would say excludes women, but I realize now this perspective is wrong. I've concluded that priests should be men, and that they should be celibate, precisely because the Church recognizes that men and women are equal, yet not the same.

Among the many difficult, dangerous jobs men do, so women don't have to, is a lifelong calling to serve God at the altar. It's a daunting commitment—a vocation that takes discipline and courage in which a man forswears becoming a husband and father to devote his life to prayer and to the Church. It isn't supposed to be easy. As we have lost reverence for the family, the magnitude of this sacrifice appears smaller to us than it should.

Joining the priesthood ought to take something away— not present the ambitious young college graduate with a path to an easy life in a grand home, with minimal work hours and a boss who looks the other way at rampant sexual misbehavior. The great demands and great seriousness of the priesthood have been diluted, which might be why feminists want women let into the club: it looks like a prize to be won.

Yes, it is baffling that an impish, occasionally foulmouthed gay Brit best known for trolling campus feminists into viral meltdowns should reflexively understand all this, and take the priesthood more seriously than a lot of people actually doing the job. But he too lives an unconventional life, and has sacrificed his physical safety, among other things, to become a truth-teller. He knows what it means to live on the edge of society for the benefit of the rest of us.

Milo was wrongly accused by the world's media in February 2017 of being "soft on pedophilia," because he'd spoken loosely about his own experiences with an abusive priest and told a few off-color jokes. I had never seen such a cruel attempt at a public execution on the basis of nothing. It shocked me. I realized what the world was prepared to do to smother unsayable truths, and how dangerous the power of laughter is to despots.

They did not break him. Milo is still fighting. His millions of fans still hang on his every word. This book is just as caustic and funny as his college talks and newspaper columns, and it reminds me of what I have always seen in Milo—a holy fool who travels the world in a tour bus with his face on it, dressed in outlandish clothes, needling his enemies with a cheeky smile and mirth in his heart.

I have been attacked by feminist colleagues for mocking their preoccupation with "straight white males." I survived because I followed the prescriptions set down in Milo's introductory memoir, *Dangerous*. Milo showed me, as he shows all of us with this new book, that rather than apologize, and tiptoe around enemy combatants, we should confront them head-on in joyful warfare. Because we are right. And because western civilization is worth saving—just as, wretched though she currently appears to us, the Bride of Christ deserves forgiveness and renewal.

PROF. RACHEL FULTON BROWN
Chicago, IL
October 2018

I.
IS THE POPE CATHOLIC?

Pope Francis has said that shepherds should have the smell of their sheep. I'll buy that. But I wonder if the stench coming from the Vatican under his tenure isn't getting a bit much. This is the story of how child abuse in the Catholic Church, which peaked decades ago, threatens to tear the Vatican apart today because Pope Francis, his accusers claim, has gone to extraordinary lengths to protect abusive priests who were personally loyal to him. It's about how decades-long guerrilla warfare between traditionalist and progressive Catholic bishops has blossomed into open civil war, prompted by explosive allegations of cover-ups by a "Lavender Mafia" of backscratching gay bishops. Yes, there really is a gay mafia, and yes, their outfits are fabulous.

It's the story of how western journalists have leapt to the defense of a pope who protected and rehired child molesters because they endorse the narrative of Francis as a reforming, left-leaning progressive. It's the story of a Church whose hierarchy has lost its way, and which desperately needs to earn back the trust of its 1.2 billion-strong following. It's about some of the changes the Church, and Christianity more generally, have undergone over the past half-century, and whether any of them might have contributed to its present crisis of moral authority. And it's also the story of what happened to me in Kent, England, in 1997, at the hands of a Catholic priest I knew as Father Michael.

Whether or not the English-speaking press wants to cover it free of political preoccupations, the latest child abuse scandal to hit the Vatican has the potential to bring down the entire Church. I'm going to tell you how we can stop that from happening, and why we should try. For all the ugly and horrifying sins of figures junior and senior in the Catholic Church, it is still a colossal force for good in the world—indeed, it is the foundation of just about everything worth preserving in Western civilization, to say nothing of its position as the sole international institution capable of resisting the rise of Islam.

There are no angels in this story, although some players certainly come out with less damning indictments than others. As documents, letters, first-hand accounts, and good old-fashioned whispering campaigns leak out of calfskin-lined ecclesiastical briefcases, the outlook for Pope Francis gets worse and worse. The fundamental facts of the story are these. Archbishop Carlo Maria Viganò, a former Vatican diplomat to the United States, has alleged that Pope Francis knew about the serial sexual harassment of seminarians by the now-degraded former cardinal Theodore McCarrick, but rehabilitated McCarrick anyway, putting him "back in circulation" after Pope Benedict XVI had placed sanctions on him that limited his movements and public activities.[1] Viganò accused Francis of "moral turpitude and doctrinal hetero-doxy," linking a dozen senior left-leaning church officials to child abuse in a long, detailed letter, and demanding that the pope step down.[2] The letter stated publicly what many have long suspected about the Vatican: that a cabal of left-wing homosexuals wield huge power within the Church hierarchy and are bringing down the entire Church by covering up for each other's odious and exploitative wrongdoing.

Theodore McCarrick's crimes have been described as "some of the worst in Church history."[3] McCarrick has intense, dark-colored eyes and a slightly hooked nose. He looks like a friendly, mischievous older relative. And that's exactly how he styled himself to his victims. To young semi-narians, he was "uncle Ted," an uncle who took his "nephews" to bed with him. The shortest man in the room, perpetually wearing a smirk, he preferred "tall, slim, intelligent" boys who did not smoke.[4] The allegations against him go back decades, were well known as far afield as England, and involve boys as young as eleven.[5] McCarrick was a voracious serial abuser, and his name was known as someone young seminarians should avoid as long ago as 1986. Six of McCarrick's victims

---

[1] https://www.scribd.com/document/387040553/TESTIMONY-of-His-Excellency-Carlo-Maria-Vigano-Titular-Archbishop-of-Ulpiana-Apostolic-Nuncio?mod=article_inline

[2] https://www.nationalreview.com/2018/09/catholic-abuse-crisis-pope-francis-owes-church-answers/

[3] https://www.churchmilitant.com/news/article/mccarricks-crimes-some-of-the-worst-in-church-history

[4] https://www.catholicnewsagency.com/news/new-allegations-surface-regarding-archbishop-mccarrick-and-newark-priests-50523

[5] https://www.firstthings.com/web-exclusives/2018/08/lessons-from-england

came forward in 2018 to allege a variety of inappropriate and illegal sexual assaults.

One account claims that in 1994, a young Irish man sent off to seminary had asked the director of priest personnel, "Has McCarrick stopped sleeping with the seminarians?" He was told: "Oh, yes, the papal nuncio and Bishop [James] McHugh both spoke to him and told him to cut it out."[6] Ten years later, three dioceses in New Jersey paid large cash settlements to keep stories about McCarrick quiet.[7] During this time, McCarrick was one of America's highest-profile Catholic priests. But until this year, the entire Vatican hierarchy, all the way up to the pope, claimed to know nothing about the allegations made against him. That's what's got people so furious. The lie isn't remotely believable, which leaves people wondering if the curia, including Francis, are laughing at them.

Why didn't American bishops do anything about their predatory peers for decades, leaving children and young men to be abused throughout the 1960s, '70s and '80s with no recourse? Viganò's letter is the first time a senior figure in the Church has broken ranks to demand answers. The Church's culture of resignation and complicity and the evident, widespread moral failings can't be ignored any longer, say commentators, many of whom were party to gossip, or were themselves abused, during that period.[8] For one thing, court settlements are starting to reach eye-watering sums, with four men awarded nearly thirty million dollars in September 2018

---

[6] http://www.bishop-accountability.org/news2006/07_08/2005_12_18_ Abbott_NewarkPriest.htm

[7] https://www.weeklystandard.com/jonathan-v-last/vigano-letter-mccarrick-wuerl-and-pope-francis-are-breaking-the-catholic-church

[8] https://www.firstthings.com/article/2018/10/catholicism-after-2018

for abuse they suffered when they were between eight and twelve years old.[9]

Needless to say, Viganò's account landed in St. Peter's Square like a lorry full of strawberry flavored condoms. I say *left-leaning* church leaders because the letter is a who's-who of Pope Francis' generals and intimates, many of the most influential left-wingers in the Church. Those who are not accused of child abuse themselves are accused of helping to brush it under the carpet, and it does seem, although there are conservatives just as guilty, that the worst offenders are precisely the same people working to dilute Church teaching on sexual matters in line with fashionable left-wing thinking. Is the conservative Archbishop Viganò's letter politically motivated? Quite possibly. But that doesn't mean his allegations aren't true. As best we can tell, not a single claim in Viganò's account has been disputed, either by journalists or those he names. Child abuse is the least appropriate political football imaginable, in which the only priority should be seeing to the needs of victims and making sure abusive priests are found and dealt with. But at least this stuff is finally coming to light.

The Catholic Church has been reeling from the effects of a liberalizing movement that began in the 1960s with a doctrinal conference called the Second Vatican Council. It was convened by Pope John XXIII, who sought to "open the windows" by modernizing the Church. But the results of Vatican II have been a disaster: an implosion of discipline and the corruption of the liturgy have created a Church that revolves around sentimentality and self-love. The Church has decayed from a place of instruction and tough love to a self-help club. Since Vatican II, most popes have been preoccupied with

---

[9] https://www.yahoo.com/news/record-27-5-mn-settlement-ny-catholic-child-022121292.html

holding together the conservative and liberal factions that emerged in its wake and which have regularly threatened to tear the Church in two.

Initially, Francis remained aloof after Viganò's bomb went off, refusing to be drawn on the subject even when asked directly by journalists. His practiced air of inscrutability has served him well in the past, but it didn't work this time, because his natural *chutzpah* got the better of him. He couldn't resist taking a swipe at his accusers in a public forum barely a week later. In a September 3 homily he told the crowd that silence makes us better imitators of Christ, as if to say: I know it looks bad, but would you all please shut up? The following week, sensing danger, he went on the offensive in another public sermon:

> In these times, it seems like the "Great Accuser" has been unchained and is attacking bishops. True, we are all sinners, we bishops. He tries to uncover the sins so they are visible, in order to scandalize the people. The "Great Accuser," as he himself says to God in the first chapter of the Book of Job, "roams the earth looking for someone to accuse."[10]

He doubled down two days later. "The only legitimate accusations that we Christians have is to accuse ourselves," he said, contrasting the Lord's invitation to be merciful with "the great accuser, Satan, who urges us to accuse others, to destroy them." It turns out sunlight isn't the best disinfectant after all. Francis has called repeatedly for "absolute transparency" in the Church's dealings, but when the allegations

---

[10] https://www.nationalreview.com/2018/09/catholic-abuse-crisis-pope-francis-owes-church-answers/

hit too close to home, suddenly he gives speeches about the devil and names sinful bishops as the true injured party.[11] You can hear the sound of jaws hitting the floor in victim support groups.

Is the pope Catholic? That's not a joke: some of us have been wondering since Francis described bishops accused of raping children, or covering up the rape of children, as "like Jesus on Good Friday," in the fourth such statement he made in the first two weeks after the Viganò letter.[12] Francis said, in his morning homily at the chapel at Santa Marta, that Jesus, in response to the cries of "crucify him," had "remained silent because he had compassion for those people deceived by the powerful."[13] The pope added: "In the same way, the pastor, in difficult times, in times when the devil is unleashed, where the pastor is accused—accused by the Great Accuser through so many people, so many powerful ones—suffers, offers his life, and prays." In his eagerness to feed conspiracies about a powerful right-wing movement out to destroy him, the pope has apparently forgotten the necessity and purpose of that most Catholic thing: confession. If these bishops have nothing to confess, they have nothing to say. But clearly they have plenty to own up to—in which case, keeping silent is a sin.

"Rome is a wreck," a senior correspondent for a Catholic magazine told me in early September 2018, "A disaster. No one knows what to do. Everyone is panicking, and those who are speaking are saying very stupid things." The Vatican under Francis has been ignoring the child abuse scandal at best,

---

[11] https://www.washingtonpost.com/national/religion/pope-francis-wants-absolute-transparency-as-he-pushes-vatican-reform/2015/02/12/92c41c20-b2d3-11e4-bf39-5560f3918d4b_story.html?utm_term=.0bfa3df3147a

[12] https://www.breitbart.com/big-government/2018/09/18/pope-francis-says-accused-pastors-are-like-jesus-on-good-friday/

[13] http://www.osservatoreromano.va/it/news/messa-santa-marta-it-2

and actively working to suppress it at worst. Its efforts have been aided by an international press that gleefully reports on Francis' veiled criticisms of Donald Trump and unsubtle references to the inefficacy of walls.[14] Journalists regard him as a heroic left-winger who says all the right things about Muslims and immigrants.[15] Immediately after the Viganò letter went public, an obviously shaken Vatican released a statement that it would respond to allegations that Pope Francis had "covered up" sexual abuse by McCarrick, which wasn't the charge Viganò had made—though, of course, it too may be true.

At the same time, allies of Francis began briefing journalists that Viganò was a "right-winger" who was driven by a grudge because he was once punished for arranging a meeting between Pope Francis and Kim Davis, the county clerk in Kentucky who made international headlines when she defied a federal court order to issue same-sex marriage licenses in August 2015. Then, without denying the main charge—that Francis had known about McCarrick's predatory behavior and Benedict's punitive sanctions, but rehabilitated him anyway—allies of the pope began wondering aloud how severe Benedict's "sanctions" had really been. They may have a point about that: it's possible Benedict was a little naïve about how effective his punishment would be at keeping McCarrick, a lifelong fame addict, out of the public eye. To protect their man, *America*'s James Martin, British journalist Austen Ivereigh and others asked publicly if those sanctions had even existed. Professor Massimo Faggioli said the idea was "not credible."[16] But eventually, Team Francis admitted

---

[14] https://www.theguardian.com/world/2017/feb/08/pope-francis-walls-bridges-donald-trump

[15] https://www.theguardian.com/world/2017/feb/08/pope-francis-walls-bridges-donald-trump

[16] https://twitter.com/matthewschmitz/status/1048973577402425344

that McCarrick had indeed been sanctioned by Benedict.[17] The sanctions were even described as "forceful."[18] At the same time, Vatican sources tried to claim that McCarrick was not an advisor to Francis, an easily disproven lie.[19] In one final, unintentionally comical touch, Cardinal Marc Ouellet, the Vatican spokesman in question, tried to defend Francis by claiming he simply wouldn't have been very interested in claims made against McCarrick.[20]

Donald Wuerl, Archbishop of Washington as I write, who assumed McCarrick's position after the latter retired in 2006, initially claimed that he knew nothing about either the crimes or the punishment of his predecessor. This is hard to believe. His first comment about the McCarrick allegations was, "I don't think this is some massive, massive crisis."[21] Perhaps Wuerl is the kind of guy so unruffled by drama that he wouldn't miss a coffee date in a nuclear apocalypse. But it's not very likely. Wuerl announced in September that he would be resigning anyway, because he has also been accused of mismanaging other past claims of clerical abuse.[22] A grand jury report claims that 1,000 children were abused by more than 300 priests over seventy years in Pennsylvania and that local bishops covered it up. Donald Wuerl, who was Archbishop of Pittsburgh at the time, is named in the report as someone who vouched for an abusive priest.[23]

---

[17] https://www.wsj.com/articles/vatican-denounces-accusation-against-pope-but-confirms-key-point-1538912551

[18] https://twitter.com/matthewschmitz/status/1048973796332462081

[19] https://twitter.com/matthewschmitz/status/1048974544948645888

[20] https://twitter.com/matthewschmitz/status/1048975147632353280

[21] https://www.youtube.com/watch?time_continue=1&v=P5RP-YvDn2E

[22] https://www.nytimes.com/2018/09/11/us/cardinal-wuerl-resigns.html

[23] https://www.nytimes.com/2018/08/14/us/catholic-church-sex-abuse-pennsylvania.html

At the same time, pontifical acolytes started offering thinly-disguised warnings to "conservative critics" which boiled down to: best leave this one alone, because there are plenty of skeletons to go around... know what I mean? None of this stopped the bleeding. There is now a consensus that Pope Francis messed up, and that he must answer the questions posed by Viganò.[24] Did he know about the allegations swirling around McCarrick and rehabilitate him anyway? Did he talk to Wuerl about it? If so, is he in the habit of looking the other way when one of his intimates is found to have done something awful? And does he think this serves a higher moral purpose, or is it merely to preserve his own power? Statements from both sides of this conflict are now coming out thick and fast.[25]

Francis's defenders have been quick to point out that the moment a credible report of abuse of a child reached the Vatican, Theodore McCarrick was publicly degraded by Francis. Degradation is the process by which a priest is stripped of his title and office; McCarrick has the distinction of being the world's only ex-cardinal. Catholics should be reassured that just as there is a saint for everything—my personal favorite being St. Gabriel Possenti, the unofficial patron saint of gun owners—so does the liturgy hold all the answers.[26] Not a happy day for Francis, I'll bet, having to stand in front of McCarrick and softly intone, *Auferimus a te baculum pastoralem, ut inde correctionis officium, quod tur-*

---

[24] https://www.thecatholicthing.org/2018/09/20/rome-failed-on-mccarrick-and-needs-to-change/

[25] https://www.thecatholicthing.org/2018/10/08/two-new-statements-and-the-Churchs-trust-deficit/

[26] https://gunowners.wordpress.com/2012/11/01/st-gabriel-possenti-patron-saint-of-gun-owners/

basti, non valeas exercere.[27] Perhaps Francis didn't actually do this. But we can daydream. In any case, the usual Francis playbook of refusing to comment, sticking it to opponents in his sermons, and then distracting the press with a left-wing stunt isn't delivering for him this time. His antagonists have drawn blood.

Perhaps Francis had never really been the PR mastermind his supporters think. For someone who enjoys holding forth on just about any subject in front of him, Francis is studiously quiet about accounts of his own misdeeds, and this silence is already being interpreted, even by priests, as guilt.[28] Maybe he's merely been coasting on left-wing privilege, insulated from tough questions by his Trump-hatred and the occasional broadside against capitalism and nationalism. Francis's response to allegations that Chilean Bishop Juan Barros Madrid, one of Francis's oldest pals, had covered up child abuse, had been to hiss, "The day someone brings me proof against Bishop Barros, then I will talk. But there is not one single piece of evidence. It is all slander. Is that clear?"[29] All Francis appeared to care about was reflexively defending an ally. Later, a 2,300-page report alleged that church officials in Chile had covered up child abuses for decades. Every active and retired bishop in Chile offered to resign, an unprecedented event in the history of the Church.

---

[27] "We take from you the pastoral staff, that hence you cannot exercise the office of correction, which you have thrown into confusion," http://wdtprs.com/blog/2018/07/history-the-rite-of-degradation-of-a-bishop/

[28] https://www.breitbart.com/big-government/2018/10/08/jesuit-priest-popes-silence-suggests-something-was-covered-up/?utm_source=newsletter&utm_medium=email&utm_term=daily&utm_content=links&utm_campaign=20181008

[29] https://www.washingtonpost.com/world/2018/10/04/chilean-church-apologizes-after-issuing-guidelines-saying-priests-shouldnt-touch-kids-genitals/?noredirect=on

Francis was eventually forced to admit he made "grave errors" handling the Chilean scandal, and 158 people are now under investigation.[30]

Pope Francis has been mired in sex scandals since the day he picked up a mitre. Twenty deaf-mute children were abused at the Provolo Institute School for the Deaf in Mendoza, Argentina, according to accusers who came forward in 2016. Five men have been arrested so far, including priests Nicola Corradi and Horacio Corbacho. Pope Francis was the bishop of Buenos Aires at the time of the alleged assaults.[31] In 2017, an Argentine woman who came forward to detail alleged abuse at the hands of a cleric in the Archdiocese of Buenos Aires, while Francis served as archbishop, accused the Pope of putting celebrity photo ops before sex crime victims. She says he was more concerned with visits from movie stars like Leonardo DiCaprio, and didn't acknowledge her complaints with so much as a letter. "I don't expect anything from him. I don't believe in him," she told a French TV station. "I suffered, and now I'm very disappointed." She is still waiting for a reply to her letters. He seems to have a fondness for disreputable figures. As Michael Brendan Dougherty writes, in an account that is by no means exhaustive:

> There is a type of churchman that Francis seems to favor: the morally compromised and the doctrinally suspect. The archbishop of Bruges, Jozef De Kesel, was known to promote the ordination of women and the making voluntary of priestly celibacy, and was credibly accused of knowingly appointing a pastor who

---

[30] https://www.cnn.com/2018/09/17/americas/pope-francis-chile-priest/index.html

[31] https://www.youtube.com/watch?v=zEvEoIIoCDY

had molested a child. Francis made him a cardinal. There was the archbishop of Stockholm, Anders Arborelius, who ignored calls to investigate a pedophile priest for years. The victim was told to go see a therapist instead. Arborelius is sympathetic to the idea of creating a female version of the College of Cardinals. Francis made him a cardinal, and Arborelius speculated that his elevation was a way for the pope to honor Sweden's commitment to refugees. There's also Giovanni Becciu, who was working for the pope's secretary of state. When the accounting firm PricewaterhouseCoopers began uncovering financial fraud in the Church, Becciu suspended its audit. The auditor general from PwC later said he was forced out on trumped-up accusations; Becciu accused that accountant of being a spy. Francis then made Becciu a cardinal. Another cleric, Archbishop Luis Ladaria Ferrer, is set to stand trial in France for his role in covering up a child-sex-abuse scandal in Lyon. Francis made him the head of the Vatican's doctrinal office, which adjudicates abuse cases.

Or consider Monsignor Battista Ricca, reportedly Francis's "eyes and ears at the Vatican Bank." Ricca was widely known for engaging in affairs with men at different posts during his clerical career. He was attacked in an area of Montevideo known for cruising, and he had to be rescued from an elevator in which he was trapped with a rent boy. (It was a question about Ricca that Francis made the occasion of his headline-grabbing statement "Who am I to judge?") And finally there is the man known as the "vice pope," Cardinal Rodríguez Maradiaga, the one being charged by seminarians in Honduras with allowing a culture of predation to flourish. Rodríguez Maradiaga first became famous across the Catholic world for saying that the Church scandals in Boston in 2002 were the invention of Jewish-controlled media who were avenging themselves on the Catholic Church for "confirm[ing] the necessity of the creation of a Palestinian state."[32]

None of this surprises people who remember Francis as Archbishop Jorge Bergoglio, who seem to understand he comes across more like a politician than a spiritual leader. In a 2010 book, *On Heaven and Earth*, Francis claimed that sexual abuse by members of the priesthood "never occurred" in his diocese, writing—the choice of words is telling—"It never happened to me." At around the same time, however, Francis had commissioned a huge study designed to pour cold water on accusations against the Church. The report speculated that "false accusers" were projecting their sexual fantasies onto innocent clergymen. Pretty audacious stuff, saying you knew nothing about sexual abuse in your diocese while commissioning a report to undermine confidence in accusers, and then comparing whistleblowers to Satan by invoking the "Great Accuser." But as the British *Spectator* magazine notes, "The duplicitous pontiff depicted by Viganò is instantly recognizable as the cynical, backstabbing Bergoglio in Henry Sire's book *The Dictator*

---

[32] https://www.nationalreview.com/magazine/2018/10/29/case-against-pope-francis-catholic-church/

Pope, which—though profoundly hostile to its subject—is based on first-hand testimony from Argentina and Rome."[33]

One of Francis's only responses to the September 2018 crisis was to invite Bono to the Vatican, so the U2 singer could later tell the press how "aghast" the pope is at the allegations against him.[34] Bono had previously dedicated a song to his "old friend" Theodore McCarrick during a concert.[35] The song was "I Still Haven't Found What I'm Looking For," whose lyrics include the following phrases, "This burning desire," "I have held the hand of a devil," and "It was warm in the night…I was cold as a stone." Whoops! Awkward.[36]

"Aghast" is an interesting choice of words, until you see Francis's actions as those of a bog-standard social justice warrior, who always doubles down on mistakes in times of crisis, and who audaciously presents his victims as the true aggressors. His social justice credentials don't end there. Consider a passage in Sire's book in which one of Francis's cronies conflates words with violence in a manner that would make a campus feminist proud, while suggesting that Francis should be beyond all criticism. Archibishop Reno Friscella, whom Francis allows to serve as President of the Council for the New Evangelization, suggests that anyone who badmouths the pope should be punished as though they had physically assaulted him, because "words, too, are rocks and stones."[37] The punishment for assaulting a pope is excommunication.

---

[33] https://www.spectator.co.uk/2018/09/what-has-pope-francis-covered-up/

[34] https://apnews.com/7c142e0af6ad49c8ad25485dcffd781d

[35] https://twitter.com/EdwardPentin/status/1042912540555206656

[36] https://www.youtube.com/watch?v=e3-5YC_oHjE

[37] Marcantonio Colonna, *The Dictator Pope: The Inside Story of the Francis Papacy* (Washington, DC: Regnery, 2018), 179.

This is a maneuver straight out of the Black Lives Matter/ Antifa playbook.[38] It is often fed to impressionable students by Marxist professors.[39] Its sophistry works in both directions. On the one hand, it means someone who merely says something you don't like deserves to be treated as a violent criminal. Conversely, when in response you smash a bike lock across someone's skull, you've not been violent, the argument goes; you've simply exercised your right to free speech. This cancer has since reached the pages of the *New York Times*, which works hard to make violent left-wing activism look respectable and justified.[40,41]

Child abuse cover-ups in the Catholic Church have proceeded in service of a culture that operates on reputation and shame, much as the modern social media-driven online mob culture does, and with oddly similar results. The compromised, the amoral, and the power-hungry have threatened, harassed, and stymied the careers of potential whistleblowers and the worst offenders have been protected at all costs. While negligent in dealing with child abuse claims, Popes John Paul II and Benedict XVI can scarcely be accused of the sort of outright complicity Francis is said to have displayed in reinstating an abusive bishop, and for the sleaziest and most disreputable reason of all: McCarrick was left-leaning, supported Francis politically, and did his bidding when called upon. John Paul's blindness may have been disastrous in the

---

[38] https://theconversation.com/justifying-the-use-of-violence-to-fight-social-injustice-is-a-recipe-for-disaster-66518

[39] https://areomagazine.com/2017/05/03/who-teaches-students-that-words-are-violence/

[40] https://www.nytimes.com/2017/07/14/opinion/sunday/when-is-speech-violence.html

[41] https://www.nationalreview.com/2017/08/free-speech-liberals-violence-argument-wrong-conflate/

long run, but he has not been accused of actively promoting the careers of abusers in the way Francis now is.

Theodore McCarrick became one of the pope's most trusted advisors, which is why Francis must be clear about what he knew of the allegations made against him, and when he learned about each of them.[42] McCarrick had shamelessly defied whatever sanctions Benedict XVI had placed on him, continuing to appear in public and give speeches. Benedict's sanctions were not only weak, it seems, but not especially well-enforced.[43] After his return to the inner circle, McCarrick bragged that Francis had put him back in business, inviting friendly journalists to report sympathetically on his churchgoer-funded globetrotting.

David Gibson of the *Religion News Service* duly obliged in June 2014 with 1,300 cloying words that described the sex abuser as a "telegenic...welcoming face" with a "twinkle in his eye" and a "sense of humor as keen as the pope's." The piece praised his "classic McCarrick style." And just in case you still weren't sure what to think of him, Gibson writes that McCarrick is "a favorite target of conservatives." That settles it! Must be a good hombre. Gibson's story was reprinted in the *National Catholic Reporter* under the vomit-inducing headline, "Globe-trotting Cardinal Theodore McCarrick is almost 84 and working harder than ever." It appeared in the *Washington Post* as well.[44]

---

[42] https://blogs.spectator.co.uk/2018/08/if-pope-francis-resigns-it-could-tear-the-catholic-church-apart/

[43] https://www.americamagazine.org/faith/2018/08/29/mccarrick-kept-robust-public-presence-during-years-he-was-allegedly-sanctioned

[44] https://www.ncronline.org/news/people/globe-trotting-cardinal-theodore-mccarrick-almost-84-and-working-harder-ever

If Viganò's claims are true, this report and the events it describes occurred a year after Viganò told Pope Francis that McCarrick had "corrupted generations of priests and seminarians." In other words, Francis knew about the allegations, yet sent his friend McCarrick out into the world anyway, to lecture young people about climate change at the laity's expense. Just a wild guess, but I'm thinking the old man doesn't fly coach. How much money was spent providing McCarrick with a globe-trotting retirement plan and regular access to young people while Francis pretended not to know about the allegations against him? In Gibson's report, McCarrick explains why he had been out of circulation recently: "Pope Benedict," he says, "was anxious to bring the Church back to where he thought it should be, and I guess I wasn't one of those who he thought would help him on that." If by "bring the Church back to where he thought it should be," McCarrick meant "make it no longer a place I can diddle kids and get rewarded with round the world plane tickets," then this is a fair gloss.

The details of the McCarrick story get more mind-bending and incredible the more you read. In 2002, U.S. bishops issued new guidelines for priests that are said to have dramatically reduced the incidence of sexual assaults. But this new "Dallas Charter" exempted bishops, and therefore cardinals, from its rules.[45] The author of these new guidelines? One Theodore McCarrick, who was exempted from the guidelines himself. They do say poachers make the best gamekeepers.

Francis's allies, who are, like him, radical left-leaning reformers, have played roles in protecting child abusers, pretending not to see what's going on or have themselves abused children. A close friend of the pope's, Cardinal Maradiaga,

---

[45] https://www.spectator.co.uk/2018/09/what-has-pope-francis-covered-up/

is accused of looking the other way when sexual harassment was going on at a seminary in Honduras. And Cardinal Godfried Danneels was infamously caught on tape in 2010 urging an abuse victim to stay silent even though the victim made specific, substantiated allegations about his own uncle, Bishop Roger Vangheluwe of Bruges. Vangheluwe admitted the assaults, saying, about a second nephew he also abused, "I had the strong impression that my nephew didn't mind at all. On the contrary. It was not brutal sex. I never used bodily, physical violence." He was convicted of sexually abusing the first boy since the age of five, but maintained, "I don't have the impression at all that I am a pedophile." Vangheluwe underwent therapy, but by 2017 he had rediscovered his mojo and has a new containment strategy: he sues anyone who comes forward to say he abused them.[46] Three years after begging abuse victims to stay silent, Vangheluwe's protector Danneels campaigned for Bergoglio's election to the papacy, and stood with him on the *loggia* when the newly elected Pope Francis was presented to the world.

Some of the statements made by close friends of Pope Francis are so heartless it's hard to believe they are real. Víctor Manuel Fernández, archbishop of La Plata, Argentina and a close friend of the pope's, has insisted that the acknowledgment of abuse claims is pointless and only feeds the "megalomania" of attention-seeking accusers, which is why Francis has said nothing about the scandal so far.[47] "[The pope] always said that it is not advisable to defend himself from people who seek the limelight, because it would give them what they seek and feed their megalomania," Fernández told

---

[46] http://www.catholicherald.co.uk/news/2017/12/13/bishop-to-sue-alleged-child-abuse-victim/

[47] https://www.breitbart.com/big-government/2018/09/18/popes-adviser-responding-to-accusers-feeds-their-megalomania/

an interviewer. "I guess that criterion applies in this case." Sadly, this kind of attitude is the norm, not the exception, in Team Francis. Fernández also accused Viganò of wanting attention, and of "acting like a teenager" in bringing the cover-up to light.[48]

Church insiders say John Paul II was better than Francis on child abuse, but it's Benedict who escapes with the least blood on his hands, though he is by no means blameless, even if his lack of action came more from paralysis and poor leadership skills than conscious mendacity and wickedness, as appears to be the case with his successor. So, this is probably not a moment for acolytes of the retired Papa Benedetto to crow—at least, not until the allegations against Benedict himself are cleared up, such as the suggestion that while an Archbishop in the 1980s he failed to heed warnings about a priest, Rev. Peter Hullerman, who forced an eleven-year-old boy to perform oral sex on him at a camp retreat in 1979 and abused several other children over the course of two decades. In July 1986, Hullerman was convicted of sexually abusing more minors and of distributing pornography.[49] He was still working with children as late as 2010.[50] Parishioners in Bad Tölz, where he was working between 2008 and 2010, described him as especially popular with children and teenagers.[51]

---

[48] http://www.periodistadigital.com/religion/america/2018/09/17/alguien-necesitado-de-un-minuto-de-falsa-gloria-iglesia-religion-dios-jesus-papa-francisco-argentina-plata-victor-fernandez.shtml

[49] http://www.spiegel.de/international/germany/sex-abuse-scandal-did-archbishop-ratzinger-help-shield-perpetrator-from-prosecution-a-684970.html

[50] http://content.time.com/time/world/article/0,8599,1973914,00.html?xid=rss-topstories

[51] https://www.nytimes.com/2010/03/16/world/europe/16church.html?mtrref=en.wikipedia.org&gwh=4CE6FE746EDCE26C83BD7C43D-425B300&gwt=pay

It remains true that the worst actors are all gay, and hard-line leftist reformers, as are the majority of those accused of looking the other way while abuse was happening. But away from the politics, this is a catastrophe that puts the Church at risk of collapse. There is a crisis of confidence brewing in the Church the likes of which it has not weathered since the Reformation. And there's no getting away from it this time by victim-blaming, ducking questions from reporters, and throwing shade at your political opponents in homilies. A case is forming against Francis that paints him as the most complicit Bishop of Rome in decades, and perhaps ever, when it comes to covering up the abuse of children and protecting others who stood by while minors were assaulted. Francis has even criticized victims' groups, accusing them of slander, before being finally shamed into staging formal investigations into Bishop Madrid.[52]

As the drama has unfurled, even mild-mannered commentators not normally known for their prurience now ask questions like, "Could the colleges in Rome, established for the education of especially promising seminarians from all over the world, in effect be gay bordellos?" Does promotion into the hierarchy "come at a price" for many of these young priests?[53] Did the Vatican invest twenty-seven million dollars into a building that housed eighteen senior priests but was also the home of Europa Multiclub, Europe's largest gay bathhouse?[54] Can it really be true, as *Vanity Fair* found

---

[52] https://www.theguardian.com/world/2018/jan/19/pope-francis-victims-church-sexual-abuse-slander-chile

[53] http://thefederalist.com/2018/08/30/pederasty-cover-will-make-civil-war-within-catholic-church/

[54] https://www.independent.co.uk/news/world/europe/as-cardinals-gather-to-elect-pope-catholic-officials-break-into-a-sweat-over-news-that-priests-share-8529670.html

in 2013, that there's a monsignor nicknamed "Jessica" who passes his business card out to twenty-five-year-old novices, and a notorious gay prostitute in Rome who poses in black leather on private balconies and in the innermost corridors of the Vatican?[55] To all of the above: Yes.

If Pope Francis knew everything Viganò alleges he did, and protected McCarrick right down to the wire anyway, it's conceivable that the modern papacy as an institution could collapse. The papacy has not adapted to modernity by developing something like Britain's parliamentary democracy: the pope has absolute authority over the Church, in the manner of a monarch from centuries past, and individual bishops wield a huge amount of power over their dioceses, because their subordinates have to swear a vow of obedience to the bishop. The Vatican may be the sole remaining world autocracy. It's certainly the most enduring and least transparent. In good times, this is an efficient form of government. But today, it presents a problem. Ordinary Catholics have lost patience with the Church's ministers, and are now openly asking what, if anything, can be done if the guy in charge refuses to discipline wayward deputies. We will return to that question later.

Francis' own allies and fans have made no secret of their reforming zeal: fangirl Austen Ivereigh, a London-based journalist, has described international summits of left-leaning churchmen meeting over a period of decades, coming to the conclusion that Francis was the man to deliver the modernization they craved. Since his election, Francis has done everything possible to sexually liberalize the Church, subverting its longstanding teachings on human sexuality. This is

---

[55] https://www.vanityfair.com/culture/2013/12/gay-clergy-catholic-church-vatican

why the Lavender Mafia was so delighted to see him sworn in. But he has also gone out of his way to excuse and cover up for friends who are guilty of the most appalling abuses of power with boys as young as eleven. The cardinals named by Viganò have done nothing to clear their names because they likely have no defense. They also know that Francis, the pervert's pope, will shelter them to the end.

II.
FATHER MICHAEL

"**L**ately, you cannot pick up a newspaper or click onto a website without encountering another mortifying story involving a priest, his penis, and a child.... Well, I'm here to defend our holy fathers. The fact of the matter is, Catholic priests have given me some of the best blow jobs of my life."[56] That's not one of mine, unfortunately. But I am well known for laughing off something awful that happened to me in the mid-1990s with tasteless jokes about kiddy-fiddling clergymen. I understand why people are confused that I'm not more torn up about it.

Worse, I enjoy making edgy jokes. I once began a college lecture for which I was dressed in a priest's collar (sorry!) with the line, "I know what you're thinking! If all priests were this hot, those little boys would stop complaining." But in the years since I came out as a victim of clerical sexual abuse, I've discovered that people who have been through what I

---

[56] https://www.salon.com/2002/05/15/holy/

went through have a wide variety of reactions to it, not all of them emotionally crippling or paralyzing. My other go-to quip used to be: "I'm not mad about what happened. If it weren't for Fr. Michael, I wouldn't give nearly such good head." That's not entirely historically accurate, as you'll learn in a moment.

I've never spoken in any detail about it before, but, for those who are interested, here are the gory details. In my mid-teens, between the ages of about thirteen and sixteen, I was member of a choir in Kent, England that met for rehearsals a few times a month. I was mourning the loss of my treble voice, having sung solos in Canterbury Cathedral to some acclaim, so I prized this hobby because it got me used to my new range. All was not lost. Life as a high baritone isn't the end of the world. It was quite a prestigious choir, and we gave some pretty big concerts. I still have a cassette tape from one of our Christmas concerts.

I had an older, bisexual friend in the choir named Alex, with whom I'd played in a band at high school. Alex introduced me to a local Catholic priest after rehearsals. He introduced Father Michael as a friend, but in such a way that I already knew something was different about him. Later, I realized that Fr. Michael had been "seeing" Alex, and that Alex was trying to escape his clutches by handing Fr. Michael some fresh meat.

It worked. On and off, over the course of about two and a half years, I was given red wine and cookies by Fr. Michael at his home while he played Rachmaninov and Gershwin on vinyl. We talked about literature and philosophy. I allowed him to perform sex acts on me. He only ever wanted to go down on me, which I was relieved about because I wasn't attracted to him, and I would have probably got the hell out of there if he'd asked for more.

If you've been to a posh boarding school, you'll know that at age fifteen, you will happily take a blow job from anyone. Plenty of rich kids cooped up with other boys for entire semesters allow the gay ones to blow them or jerk them off. That's how it felt with Fr. Michael. I liked getting off, and he liked doing it, and I didn't think much more of it, except obviously that I should keep lying to my mom about visiting friends after choir. I've since been emailed, after dropping just enough information in public that fellow victims could be sure they had been preyed upon by the same man, and it turns out he did a lot more with other boys, so I got off lightly. (Obviously, my first thought was: Wait, what? Did he think I was ugly or something?) And I've learned that some of the boys who spent time with Fr. Michael came out of it a lot more emotionally battered than I did, so I have come to take the whole thing more seriously, and realize that what happened was abusive and wrong.

Because Fr. Michael is now dead—the old cunt hanged himself rather than face trial when one of his other boys went public, and his cowardice in killing himself offends me even more than what he did to me—I never felt any obligation to go public with my story until I was forced to, as you probably recall, in a globally-televised press conference from New York in February 2017.[57] That's when the establishment right and mainstream media teamed up to take me out, pretending that I was a "supporter of pedophilia" because I'd made a few off-color jokes about Fr. Michael and about clerical abuse in general.

It was a disingenuous hit job, designed to knock me down a peg or two because I was a rising star who hated the Right and Left Establishments equally, and because I was an influential public supporter of Donald Trump. What they did felt

---

[57] https://www.youtube.com/watch?v=ABJo7w-efTA

worse, to me, than anything that timid, slightly pathetic old man in Kent might have done to me. They accused me of being an apologist for a crime of which I was the victim. They pretended I was serious when I called abuse victims "whinging little brats." I wasn't serious. Of *course* I wasn't serious. It's just that, in the moment, I found it amusing, and shocking, and a funny thing to say. I did make one remark I regret, about the age of consent being "arbitrary," but they never show the whole video, where I go on to say that I think the current legal age is about right and that sexual relations must always be consensual.[58] That sets me apart from many supposedly respectable gay lobby groups, which never face criticism for arguing that the age of consent should be lower.

As a writer and speaker, I insist that no joke is off limits to me, and I take exception to people who suggest I can't joke about my own experiences. If nothing else, don't they realize it's the best way to cope? I know what they'd prefer, of course. They'd rather I cried and yelled and fell apart at the mere sight of the cross and demanded a safe space from Catholicism so the thought of being bent over an altar didn't trigger me. But that's just not how I feel about it, and I can't pretend that it is.

I am a public figure who occasionally says awful things about other people, so I'm in no position to play the victim. But I do feel a bit aggrieved about how I had to stand up in front of the world's media, streamed live on CNN and Fox News, and tell the whole planet that I'd been sexually assaulted as a young man. I had never felt any great shame or embarrassment about it until I had to do that. And I hate that my now-husband John, whom I'd known for less than six months at the time, had to find out that way, too. I'd

---

[58] https://heavy.com/news/2017/02/milo-yiannopolous-pedophilia-tran-script-pederasty-video-full-sex-boys-men-catholic-priest-cpac-quotes/

mentioned Fr. Michael in public before, but never in front-page-national-news context. John had made it clear at the start of our relationship that he wasn't going to watch any of my speeches or read any press about me, by which I was relieved. I've never forcibly outed anyone else's private griefs like that, and I've done some aggressive reporting from the front lines of the culture wars.

I'm not *glad* all this happened to me, obviously, even though I always get big laughs for the pedo priest jokes at my shows. But it simply wasn't the most awful thing I've had to endure. I've been in far greater distress at other times in my life. And when I met another, similarly lonely old man, who became my journalistic mentor for a while and also wanted a sexual relationship with me, I think my experience with Fr. Michael better prepared me to set down clear ground rules for our interactions. When my friendship with him became conditional on sex—some seven years after we'd first met—I put an immediate stop to it.[59]

On the other hand, I know that acting on your gay urges—"deciding to be a gay man"—isn't entirely genetic. A lot of factors go into it, some of them inherited, some of them environmental. Did my experience with Fr. Michael push me in one direction or the other? It's hard to say. On one hand, if you think about it, it was more likely to repel me into being straight. He was no Reggie Bush. But perhaps by offering a weird father-surrogate with a sexual component, he shaped my development toward same-sex attraction. I couldn't tell you. If I somehow knew for sure that without my experiences in his living room all those years ago that I'd be happily married with children, I'd have spared him the trip to Home Depot for rope and finished him off myself.

---

[59] https://www.dangerous.com/36684/milo-sexually-harassed-by-journalistic-mentor/

That would be truly injurious, a sin against another person that could never be forgiven. But I am happy—truly content—in my marriage. I couldn't imagine life without John. So, you see, it's all very complicated and there aren't any straightforward answers.

If I hadn't been forced to come out like that, I would never have sought out recollections and testimonies from other victims. I thought I was a weirdo for feeling somewhat responsible for what happened, because I recall at that age, in my mid-teens, getting a kick out of sexual attention from older men. I found it flattering. I didn't have a male role model at home because dad was gone and my mom's new husband was an ogre. Getting affirmation from a male authority figure—in whatever form it came—felt good. Abusers often seek out kids with weak family ties like I had.[60] I was a sexually precocious teenage boy who wanted to see and do everything, including, though it makes me laugh to even think of it now, girls.

All three of the girls I dated at the time are dead now, from overdose, car accident, and suicide respectively. That's not a joke, because it's true. I like to make the excuse that I couldn't go straight now, even if I wanted to, because I couldn't live with the body count. That's what I thought I was doing, joking about Fr. Michael in those college talks: making light of a serious subject to take away its power to hurt me. And you know what? Fuck anyone who says I can't. I will never stop making jokes about, well, just about anything I please. Like the fact that it's not just the Catholic Church where these male predators operate. I had sex with one of my English teachers, too, and no, I don't want to talk about it.

---

[60] https://www.wfaa.com/article/news/two-child-sex-offenders-explain-how-they-picked-their-targets/287-434667495

Earlier, I mentioned my husband, as though it's no big deal that a Catholic man—and a self-described traditionalist, at that—should have a "husband." Don't worry. I'm not under any illusions that my marriage is legitimate in the eyes of God. I'm not about to dispute the Church's teachings on homosexuality, because I wouldn't dream of demanding that she throw away her hard truths just so I can feel better about myself. But I do think that if I'm going to sin, I should do so in a way that's as close to living virtuously as possible. And, you know, tax breaks.

You may have intuited by now that I'm not afraid of being imperfect or shocking. As I told the Jesuit journal *America*, in an interview it was too timid to publish, and from which I borrow here, plenty of the saints were shocking, to say nothing of our Lord.[61] And shocking is in the eye of the beholder. I find the current pope pretty shocking, for instance. I'm also shocked by supposedly Catholic politicians who make laws in flat contradiction to the natural law. So, while I understand readers who may be skeptical of my qualifications to opine on the state of the Church, let me remind you what we normally call wealthy, self-absorbed, cross-dressing, gay Catholics wearing too much gold jewelry: "Your Eminence."

I like to joke about my lack of chastity—at least, I used to. I'm getting closer to Augustine's "yet" every day. (His famous prayer was, "Lord, make me chaste. But not yet.") But for every joke that makes you wince, remember that I supported Paul VI's criticism of artificial contraception so strongly that Hillary Clinton attacked me for it during her presidential campaign.[62] Isn't it alarming that I, a poor sinner, have spoken out more forcefully and more effectively on contraception than 99 percent of our bishops?

---

[61] https://www.churchmilitant.com/news/article/the-catholic-magazine-interview-with-milo-they-refuse-to-print

[62] https://www.youtube.com/watch?v=36VU0LUUJwE

Evelyn Waugh liked to make an observation I often quote: "Protestants seem to think, I'm good, therefore I go to church, whereas Catholics think, I'm very bad, therefore I go to Church." Oscar Wilde thought differently: "The Catholic Church is for saints and sinners alone. For respectable people the Anglican Church will do." I've never been in any doubt which of those groups I belong to. Waugh also said, when people asked how he could possibly call himself a Catholic: "You have no idea how bad I'd be if I weren't." That pretty much sums up my feelings on the subject.

Yes, I have sex with my husband, but as a Catholic I know there are far worse sins than lust. Sins of the flesh are at the bottom of the scale of wrongdoing, because they merely involve improperly calibrated love directed at otherwise "good objects," as Dante says.[63] The Church says self-righteousness is at the top of the pile of sins. I'm pretty confident that by that measure, I'm in a lot better shape than my feminist and Establishment Republican enemies, and, for that matter, a lot better shape than some of the cardinals we'll meet in these pages. Not for nothing were some of the strongest punishments in Church legislation reserved for those who abuse children and adolescents.[64] We'll return to the gay question in a future chapter, where I'll explain why your parish priest is probably gay and what we can do to make the Vatican straight again.

Growing up Catholic taught me the value of humility, and though it's not a virtue I practice as often as I should, it's an important principle because it teaches us to tolerate other opinions. Often, our enemies have things to teach us, even if

---

[63] https://www.jstor.org/stable/pdf/3720152.pdf

[64] Matthew Cullinan Hoffman, *The Book of Gomorrah and St. Peter Damian's Struggle Against Ecclesiastical Corruption* (New Braunfels, TX: Ite ad Thomam Books, 2015), 18.

they don't mean to. It is only through humility that we can grow, because without humility we don't listen properly to what other people tell us. In the course of writing this book, and speaking to more fellow victims, I have realized that not everyone is able to shrug off what happened to them like I did. That's one of the reasons I've written it, not only to lay the media storm around me to rest, at last, but also to play a small part in helping to reform an institution I cherish and depend upon. If this book contributes to a new atmosphere of zero tolerance for sex pests in the clergy, I've done my job. The rest is between me and God.

People ask me, sometimes in amazement, "How can you be Catholic?" What they really mean is, "Why don't you affirm every tiny detail of your life and then demand that the world validate your self-aggrandizement?" This is very stupid. The fact that I am a Catholic means that I begin from the objective truth of God's existence and love, from which it follows that I am not perfect. I'm heartened by a passage in Lunn and Lean's *Cult of Softness*, which could have been written about Team Francis: "The pride which the Church condemns is the pride which is prevalent in this age of atheistic humanism, the rejection of absolute standards, and the substitution of Self for God as the judge of one's own actions… Only the great saints have consistently practiced what they preached. The trouble with the modern world is that too many influential people preach what they practice."[65]

This is the last time I'll ever mention Fr. Michael's name, except as the punchline to a joke. He's had enough of my time already—and so have people who keep bringing up the subject. Except to say, credit where it's due, he really did give good blow jobs.

---

[65] Arnold Lunn and Garth Lean, *The Cult of Softness* (London: Blandford Press, 1965)

III.
ENEMY OF THE PEOPLE

Instances of child abuse in the Catholic Church have been dropping precipitously for decades in the United States. I won't be so rash as to claim that it doesn't happen anymore, but, statistically speaking, the problem of child sexual abuse in the Church already appears to be correcting itself, or at least rapidly falling into line with other, similar organizations from its peak between 1965 and 1980. One question you might ask is, why are we still hearing about this? Or, more specifically, why are we only hearing about this now?

The main reason abuse claims and reporting about them trail the offenses by decades is that victims often take decades to speak out about their experiences. Usually, they pipe up in their mid-thirties.[66] That was certainly the case for me, and although I can't speak for other victims, I have a pretty good idea why it might be that people don't tell their stories until

---

[66] http://nineteensixty-four.blogspot.com/2018/08/pain-never-disap-pears-from-unhealed.html

much later in life. I don't think it's because anyone who ever got fiddled with has been so utterly traumatized by it that he's been unable to function as a human being ever since. Doubtless for some victims that's the case, and my heart goes out to them. But they are in the minority.

What I think's really going on is that by thirty, you have enough else going on in your life that disclosing the embarrassing fact that a priest years ago did something inappropriate to you isn't going to define your life. By thirty-five, you hopefully have a family of your own through whom your identity is forged, and who can provide some emotional support. The unfortunate minority who are permanently crippled by their child abuse experiences have, understandably I suppose, permitted it to define them—so much so that their entire being has become an expression of the trauma. I've known rape victims both male and female, and I think the same thing is going on here.

Another explanation for the delay we've experienced in hearing about abuse that peaked in the '60s, '70s, and '80s is the reliably useless finger-in-the-ear approach from the Church hierarchy which, under Francis, has ascended to the status of a systematic cover-up at the very highest levels, at the expense of victims past and present, in service to the continued power of a small group of cardinals and bishops, including the pope himself. But it's not just that there are powerful homosexuals covering for each other. The structures and operations of the Vatican are riddled with bureaucracy and corruption that prevent vital reforms. Just like any other city in which power and money are concentrated, the Vatican is rife with plots, backstabbing, and rivalry. But the usual skullduggery and jostling for position that go on in, say, Washington, D.C., are elevated to theatrical levels of intrigue because the stakes are so high. After all, he who controls the Vatican controls the Catholic Church, and thus commands spiritual authority over 1.2 billion people. And there's an awful lot of money sloshing around, too, in relatively few hands.

Anyone with experience with the inner workings of the Vatican describes it as comically ineffective and dysfunctional, the product of a thousand schemes that make critical documents disappear at just the right moment and accountability practically impossible. Add to that the Vatican's way of dealing with sensitive matters, which often leaves no paper trail, and you have a recipe for chaos, easily exploitable by well-connected sociopaths who can command the loyalty of the curia, whether through ideological fealty or straight intimidation. As Kurt Martens, professor of canon law at The Catholic University of America, explains, "Rome often works with oral reports, and that makes it harder," he said. "It's the Italian way of dealing with these things, especially when they involve a cardinal or a bishop."[67] This may be one reason Viganò's allegations prove difficult to substantiate—or to disprove.

Corruption and misappropriation of funds are standard operating procedure in Rome. In September 2018, the Vatican confirmed that the Sistine Chapel choir's manager and director were being investigated for money laundering, fraud, and embezzlement.[68] Profits from concerts are said to have been paid directly into an account held by manager Michelangelo Nardella and director Mgr. Massimo Palombella, and used for personal expenses. Palombella is also under investigation for abusive conduct during choir rehearsals. By Vatican standards, that's J.V. level stuff. Exhibit A: The Vatican Bank.

---

[67] https://www.americamagazine.org/faith/2018/08/29/mccarrick-kept-robust-public-presence-during-years-he-was-allegedly-sanctioned

[68] http://www.catholicherald.co.uk/news/2018/09/13/vatican-confirms-ongoing-inquiry-into-sistine-chapel-choir-finances/

The Vatican Bank is one of the most disreputable and ineptly-managed financial institutions in the world. For decades, it operated as a tax haven for wealthy Italians and as a money-launderer's paradise. It is essentially an offshore bank in the middle of Rome, subject to its own laws and was therefore—for a while—resistant to demands for information from the Italian authorities, not themselves always the perfect model of good governance.[69] International media scrutiny of the bank is said to be one of the reasons Benedict XVI resigned, admitting privately to friends that he was unable to tackle the entrenched special interests in Rome.

After taking some time to admire Francis for wearing a plastic watch and dining in the Vatican canteen, *The Guardian's* Paul Vallely has given a decent account of how Cardinal George Pell, appointed by Francis, began a review of the bank's operations. Pell had successfully overhauled the Church's finances in Sydney and Melbourne. The Australian son of a former heavyweight boxer, Pell is a political and doctrinal conservative who speaks aggressively and does not believe in man-made climate change. He is a cult hero among conservative Catholics. You can imagine what the Lavender Mafia think of him. Vallely notes grudgingly that, "For all his conservatism, Pell had for years been a vocal critic of the Roman Catholic bureaucracy and its corruption."

Pell moved quickly, and made enemies. A straight dealer to the point of unbearable bluntness, especially in the delicately perfumed and gold-embroidered world of the Holy See, Pell probably didn't anticipate getting tripped up by dirty tactics: in this case, stories leaked to the media about—you guessed it—clerical abuse. The press reports were coincidentally timed, arriving just as Pell's reforms of the bank began

---

[69] https://www.theguardian.com/world/2015/aug/13/can-pope-francis-clean-up-gods-bank

to take hold. It was alleged that Pell was soft on child abuse, thanks to offhand comments he had made years before, in typically ribald and direct Australian fashion. It was suggested that he may himself have some questions to answer about covering up abuse. Then the allegations widened, to direct accusations of historic sex abuse, at which point Pell had to put his work at the bank on hold. Now Pell is back in Australia, trying to clear his name, and his reforms are stalling, just as the intriguers intended. This is how efforts to clean up the Roman Catholic Church usually end.

Another factor to consider in the delay between these abuses and us hearing about them now is how incompetently the media covers religion. For a subject as critical not just to world affairs but to Western civilization generally, religion is poorly served by establishment reporters. Very few British newspapers have dedicated religion correspondents any longer, and where religion is covered nationally in the United States it is almost always subservient to the political agenda of the masthead, with reporting from people who know hilariously little about their subject. With a few exceptions, publications aimed at millennials are execrably bad at reporting on religious subjects, perhaps because there are literally no Christians on staff at all. Though she makes no effort to hide her leftist politics, *Vox*'s Tara Isabella Burton at least makes an effort to understand the views of her subjects, and seems to know her beat.[70] But her stablemates at *Vox* merrily hold forth on religion without the slightest grasp of basic facts.

We are now in the remarkable position that national newspapers in America publish lead stories about religion that contain glaring howlers, because there is no one left in the building with any domain expertise whatsoever. You'd be

---

[70] https://www.vox.com/2017/10/14/16468878/milo-yiannopoulos-trash-talks-pope-in-catholic-magazine-interview

hard-pressed to find anyone working for a major TV news channel who knows what a papal nuncio is. My favorite example of this in action is the *New York Times* reporter who asked Christian writer and editor Fr. Richard John Neuhaus of *First Things* what he made of the fact that the newly elected pope was "also" going to be named the bishop of Rome.

Christianity in general and Catholicism in particular are impossibly complex subjects for a general reporter to master in an afternoon, but because reporters, editors, and proprietors are mostly Democrat and mostly secularist, religion has been one of the first areas to go when newsroom cuts have been made over the past decade. Unless it's pandering to Islam to annoy Republicans, they just don't want to know. So, we are left with specialist magazine writers, all of whom have their particular biases and objectives. Perhaps the only reason this latest conflagration captures the attention of English-speaking journalists is that they've identified a way to bash conservatives in the story by pointing out Viganò's political leanings, and because any kind of sexual abuse story is grounds for an otiose pivot back to the #MeToo movement and another 400 words about the evils of patriarchy.

In matters of theology and the complex arena of Church politics, journalists do what they do in any situation where the facts are too exhausting and time-consuming to uncover: they go with the guy the conservatives hate, which in this case means siding with McCarrick and Francis. As Ben Shapiro points out, "The media have rushed to Francis's defense… Because Francis is widely perceived to share leftist sensibilities regarding issues like climate change, illegal immigration, and homosexuality. The media believes…that the abuse of children is of lower priority than climate change and illegal immigration. Furthermore, they fear that focus will be placed on a homosexual subculture within the church, some of whose participants have been linked with molestation."[71]

It's possible that journalists genuinely don't know what all the fuss is about. After all, so many of their own idols are pederasts. As the great firebrand Anthony Esolen, writing for *Crisis* magazine, reminds us, San Francisco Supervisor Harvey Milk, the first openly gay elected official in the U.S., groomed and seduced young boys but was turned by the Left into a civil rights hero.[72] Harry Hay, Allen Ginsberg, and William S. Burroughs are all taught in literature courses. All three were blatant and proud pederasts. *Lolita* and *Death in Venice* are both considered great literature. The old boys of the Left covered endlessly for Sir John Gielgud. R. Kelly's exile lasted minutes. Roman Polanski was given the red carpet treatment on his way back into the tent. And that's before we get to the decades of la-la-la-I'm-not-listening it took to keep Kevin Spacey's cocaine-fueled indiscretions with young men out of the press, or to hush up *Guardians of the Galaxy* director James Gunn's obsession with sexualized images of children and his creepy blog, on which he has bragged about beating up his midget girlfriend.[73]

But if the media doesn't *really* care about sex with minors, they gleefully assaulted this author when he dared to make a few jokes about his own experiences and speak frankly about a few facts of gay life. It couldn't be, could it, that in fact they care nothing at all for the victims of child sex abuse, and instead use this emotive subject merely to destroy their

---

[71] https://www.dailywire.com/news/35195/medias-coverage-pope-francis-alleged-sex-abuse-ben-shapiro

[72] https://www.crisismagazine.com/2018/what-the-priest-scandal-is-and-is-not-about

[73] https://www.dangerous.com/48296/revealed-james-gunn-bragged-about-beating-up-his-midget-girlfriend-for-not-fitting-into-mini-fridge/

political opponents? That pederasty is only bad when conservatives do it, and then it's so bad that *merely joking about something that happened to you personally* is enough to get you machine-gunned? I won't believe it!

But how, then, to explain the behavior of the mainstream press this past year? Everything journalists have done in reporting this crisis has been to protect the reputation of a pope perceived as a leftist, and to save the feelings of the homosexual lobby, which hates it when gay people are talked about honestly in public as the promiscuous, low-income, drug-taking, reckless, and unhappy people we (statistically) are. The cover-up in the Vatican is a gay crime, performed by gay men in service of other gay men, concerning assaults overwhelmingly performed by men on young boys and a debased culture of gay orgies in what ought to be educational establishments. In the Catholic world, gay scandals have a habit of multiplying—and not just because young male seminarians tessellate.

And it's not just a gay crime: it's a predominantly left-wing gay crime, with the perpetrators more likely than not to be "hippy-dippy, loosey-goosey innovators with the liturgy, heterodox on family matters, and very bad managers of diocesan resources, especially the schools."[74] In the long run, no amount of soft-pedaling from the *Times* is going to obscure the fact that the corrupt, socialist, homosexual mafia in charge of the Holy See is a disease which, left untreated, will destroy the Catholic Church. Maybe that's the plan. But the rest of us aren't going to stand by and watch it happen.

You can imagine the panic at the *New York Times* when a scandal erupts and it looks like all the bad guys are left-wing gays whose Google result pages show a bunch of speeches

---

[74] https://www.crisismagazine.com/2018/what-the-priest-scandal-is-and-is-not-about

about climate change and embracing migrants. Whatever can be published to distract attention from the perpetrators is hastily cobbled together for the morning edition. Take this *Times* headline from August 2018, which appeared in print as, "Francis Takes High Road As Conservatives Pounce, Taking Criticisms Public." Online, the *Times* headlined the story, "Vatican Power Struggle Bursts Into Open As Conservatives Pounce." Here's how the story begins:

> Since the start of his papacy, Francis has infuriated Catholic traditionalists as he tries to nurture a more welcoming church and shift it away from culture war issues, whether abortion or homosexuality. "Who am I to judge?" the pope famously said, when asked about gay priests.
>
> Just how angry his political and doctrinal enemies are became clear this weekend, when a caustic letter published by the Vatican's former top diplomat in the United States blamed a "homosexual current" in the Vatican hierarchy for sexual abuse. [75]

In case that's too subtle for readers, embedded in the page before the main body of the story even starts is a video of Francis with all that "who am I to judge" malarkey about queers, so *Times* readers are left in no doubt who the bad guys are. Elsewhere the same day, Reuters published a story with the headline, "Defenders rally around Pope, fear conservatives escalating war." [76]

---

[75] https://www.nytimes.com/2018/08/27/world/europe/vatican-power-struggle-bursts-into-open-as-conservatives-pounce.html

[76] https://www.reuters.com/article/us-pope-abuse-escalation/defenders-rally-around-pope-fear-conservatives-escalating-war-idUSKCN1LD27Y

The media's protection of Francis worked for a while, most notably in the early, myth-building period of his papacy. As recently as November 2017, the *Washington Post* was still running headlines such as, "How Pope Francis Can Cleanse The Far-Right Rot From The Catholic Church."[77] That aged well! Catholic news services have expressed surprise on the rare occasion a mainstream outlet has covered alleged wrongdoing by Francis without smothering the reporting in defensive language or vague gesturing toward a conservative conspiracy.[78] Pope Francis enjoyed remarkably high approval ratings among Americans for some time. But down from a peak of two-thirds in early 2017, only 48 percent of Americans have a favorable view of Pope Francis as of September 2018, because no amount of spin can obscure the facts. Among Catholics, the number is 63 percent, down from 83 percent.[79]

Among Republicans, Francis's approval sits at just 36 percent in a CNN poll.[80] A second Gallup poll showed a similarly low approval rate among the general American population of just 53 percent, a sharp downturn.[81] The pope's approval rating is expected to drop further, with women abandoning their previous fondness for Francis at the most rapid rate out of all demographic groups—the maternal

---

[77] https://www.washingtonpost.com/news/global-opinions/wp/2017/02/09/how-pope-francis-can-cleanse-the-far-right-rot-from-the-catholic-church/?noredirect=on&utm_term=.12f049a7d439

[78] https://www.lifesitenews.com/news/mainstream-media-catch-up-ap-publishes-story-on-popes-cover-up-as-arch

[79] http://www.catholicherald.co.uk/news/2018/09/13/pope-franciss-popularity-plummets-among-americans-according-to-poll/

[80] https://edition.cnn.com/2018/09/12/politics/pope-francis-poll/index.html

[81] https://news.gallup.com/poll/242216/pope-francis-favorability-down-sharply.aspx

instinct finally kicking in. Now even *Der Spiegel*, the left-wing German magazine besotted with Francis, has turned on the old man. A dramatically illustrated cover story in late 2018 broke with hagiographic tradition by describing Francis as an "ice-cold, cunning Machiavellian" who "often speaks at inopportune moments, yet in important moments remains silent."[82] The magazine stated, with unusual directness: "He lies." Its cover carried the phrase: "Du sollst nicht Lügen."[83] Eventually, even journalists are forced to tell the truth.

First Things editor Rusty Reno suggests that the lingering cover-up culture in America might have been made possible because America's bishops began the nineteenth century unusually powerful and autonomous. Their authority wasn't limited by hundreds of years' worth of Catholic institutions such as libraries, faculties, and cathedral chapters, and they were not subject to European canon law.[84] American bishops have acted more independently of Rome than their European counterparts. Some journalists conclude that, combined with the bishop-centric Church structure that was obtained after Vatican II, abuses in America have gone unpunished thanks to cowardice and poor oversight from Rome. But it appears that the Vatican knew what was happening all along and simply did nothing about it or feigned ignorance, a trend that has reached its apotheosis under Pope Francis.

One last note about the delay: Thomas Sowell has observed that any given social problem typically becomes a focus of attention and government action only well after the problem is significantly improving—usually with the effect

---

[82] https://magazin.spiegel.de/SP/2018/39/159553179/index.html?utm_source=spon&utm_campaign=centerpage

[83] https://www.breitbart.com/national-security/2018/09/24/vatican-cardinal-pope-francis-ice-cold-cunning-machiavellian/

[84] https://www.firstthings.com/article/2018/10/catholicism-after-2018

of retarding progress. Certainly, this has been the case in the "campus rape crisis" of the last half-decade, an outpouring of confected rage about perhaps the safest public spaces for women anywhere in the western world, at a time when rape rates are in freefall, and have been for years. The Church and the media follow this rule now when it comes to clerical sexual abuse, reluctantly opening investigations when the worst offenses are already half a century old, and the statute of limitations has long since passed, virtually guaranteeing that victims will see no justice and no compensation for their ordeals.

If all that hasn't depressed you enough about the moral ruins of the Catholic Church, consider another reason Francis ferociously protected Theodore McCarrick, how the most morally indefensible decisions by the Vatican come to be made, and why it takes decades to bring some of these men to justice, long after the victims can have their proper day in court. McCarrick, you see, was one of the Church's most effective fundraisers, helping to establish a Papal Foundation in 1988 whose assets have grown to over two hundred million dollars.[85] The Foundation built $70,000 schools in Bangladesh, $90,000 libraries in Nicaragua, and $100,000 orthopedic units in Ghana, many projects coming with a nice overseas junket for McCarrick.

Everything was going swimmingly until the summer of 2017, when Pope Francis personally requested an immediate grant of twenty-five million dollars, one hundred times higher than the usual grant size, for a Church-owned hospital in Rome that is notoriously corrupt. Rod Dreher, writing for the *American Conservative*, reported that the hospital has been accused of money laundering and has liabilities of more than one billion dollars. This is not normal. The Papal

---

[85] https://www.theamericanconservative.com/dreher/sex-money-clericalism-papal-foundation/

Foundation, which is maintained by wealthy Americans, does not invest in this kind of project and had been given no opportunity to perform due diligence on the hospital. But the bishops and cardinals on its board—led by none other than Cardinal Wuerl from Washington—forced through a wire transfer for half the money a few days after the request came in. What was the money really for? And where did it go? We will probably never find out.

When Francis was informed that the other half of the grant would not be forthcoming, he responded with spectacular pettiness: he cancelled the board's annual audience with him at the Vatican. The plot thickens still further when you discover that one board member, Tim Busch, is friends with the author of the letter that began this whole scandal in the first place: Archbishop Viganò. "Might this be a case of telling the truth about sex as payback for arrogant senior clerics pushing around the laity and picking their pockets?" asks Dreher.

For all its rapacious acquisition of wealth, the money the Vatican does manage to collect from naïve donors is spent so haphazardly, and accounted for so incompetently—or, more likely, dishonestly—that it makes you wonder why they bother in the first place. But to understand as a lay Catholic just how badly the Church spends your money, you first have to understand how thoroughly the organization was co-opted decades ago by communist activists. Yes, you read that right.

Despite popular myth, the Church has never been a friend to European fascism: John Cornwell's malicious and error-strewn 1999 bestseller *Hitler's Pope*, which was, of course, warmly received by the media, was a libel on the legacy of Pius XII. It helped to solidify the myth of the Catholic church as a sinister, Nazi-sympathizing, right-wing organization.[86] In fact, we now know that Pius XII's actions in Italy and via diplomats throughout Eastern Europe could have saved as many as 850,000 Jewish lives. Would Hollywood ever make *Pius's List?*

But the Church has often been a willing vessel for communism, to the point of convergence. To the surprise of some non-Catholics, the Church has always been a somewhat left-leaning institution. We did, after all, invent the concept of social justice. There is a long history of infiltration of the churches by communist sympathizers, activists, and spies. In many cases, this occurred with the co-operation of priests. In the 1930s, communists in the West were told to rejoin churches and other Western institutions to begin weakening them from the inside. The Communist Party's infiltration into Catholic seminaries was designed to turn the church from a spiritual hierarchy to a more explicitly political organization, with the goal of weaponizing it, encouraging the religious poor across the world to rebel against the "institutionalized violence of poverty."[87] In 1968, as the clerical abuse crisis was reaching its zenith, the KGB-created Christian Peace Conference persuaded leftist South American bishops to hold a conference in Colombia to explore Marxist liberation ideology.

Communists not only sought to leverage the Church against capitalism—the most effective engine of social mobility the human species has yet devised—in the name of alleviating poverty. They also aimed to enfeeble the most powerful institutions of liberal Western capitalist democracies, such as universities and the press. There is no higher calling to

---

[86] http://www.catholicherald.co.uk/issues/march-10th-2017/the-end-of-the-hitlers-pope-myth/

[87] http://www.lepantoinstitute.org/cchd/the-marxist-core-of-the-catholic-campaign-for-human-development/

a Leninist than weakening the system upon which Western civilization is based: Christianity, and especially in its most potent Roman form. The Catholic Church was identified by communists as more important to the success of the West even than the means of production: Saul Alinsky, author of the activist handbook *Rules for Radicals*, identified the "two basic social forces which might serve as the cornerstone of any effective community organization" in 1980s Chicago as "first, the Catholic Church, and second, organized labor."[88]

The pro-abortion and pro-birth control Alinsky had lifelong friendships and working relationships with many Catholic priests, especially in Chicago, some of whom raised large sums of money for a project that came to be known as the Catholic Campaign for Human Development. The "Catholic" was added later, in typical Marxist fashion, because the CHD was acquiring a reputation for funding causes that ran directly contrary to Church teaching. Alinsky proudly explains his bamboozlement of the Catholic hierarchy in *Rules for Radicals*. Alinsky's CCHD is still active today, still endorsed by the United States Conference of Catholic Bishops, and still collects money from ordinary Catholics that it funnels into pro-abortion and pro-contraception groups under the guise of "anti-poverty" and "racial healing" initiatives, thanks to a combination of complicity and naïveté from Church leaders.[89]

To this day, hundreds of ordained ministers support outright Marxist organizations in America, and there are deep

[88] https://digitalcommons.wayne.edu/cgi/viewcontent.cgi?referer=http://www.lepantoinstitute.org/cchd/the-marxist-core-of-the-catholic-campaign-for-human-development/&httpsredir=1&article=1024&context=csr

[89] http://www.usccb.org/about/catholic-campaign-for-human-development/

ties between Church officials and far-left political activist groups such as the Democratic Socialists of America.[90] The Syracuse Cooperative Federal Credit Union receives funding from the CCHD despite supporting gay marriage and donating money to Planned Parenthood.[91] It's this sort of self-defeating stupidity and lack of moral fortitude and consistency that political activists can exploit to dilute the effectiveness of a large organization like the Church. In her last book, conservative hero Phyllis Schlafly reprinted documents which show that Barack Obama received his community organizer training in 1986 at Alinsky's Industrial Areas Foundation, courtesy of the Archdiocese of Chicago.[92] Although it's true that communists did not fully infiltrate the American Catholic Church—even communists have standards—they have had enormous influence on the Church in Latin America. Critic Henry Sire notes that there's a cultural component to Latin American Catholicism that may have led to Francis' habitual blindness about the moral corruption of his lieutenants.[93]

It's easy to see why prelates from a centralized religion might be statists, assuming that human beings need an overbearing economic and legal authority to complement their organized spiritual shepherding. And the Catholic Church's close association with communists goes all the way to the top. In September 2018, Francis signed a deal with the Chinese government that codified Communist Party interference in

---

[90] http://www.lepantoinstitute.org/cchd/the-marxist-core-of-the-catholic-campaign-for-human-development/

[91] http://www.cooperativefederal.org/files/50%20-%20Spring%2002.pdf

[92] https://www.lifesitenews.com/news/catholic-bishops-helped-to-fund-alinsky-training-for-barack-obama-according

[93] https://audioboom.com/posts/7000843-what-has-pope-francis-covered-up

the selection of Chinese bishops.[94] The deal not only grants the Chinese power to nominate bishops, but also requires the Vatican to recognize seven excommunicated bishops currently operating without papal consent in China. This deal makes China the only country in the world in which the pope's authority to select bishops is circumscribed by state authorities—and China isn't even a Catholic country.[95] Persecution of Catholics in China is "at its highest level since the Cultural Revolution," according to human rights campaigners.[96] Long-time missionary and China expert Fr. Sergio Ticozzi told journalists the same month that the Chinese government seeks "absolute control" over the Catholic Church.[97] This agreement brings them closer to it, and with legitimacy derived from the Holy See itself. Matthew Schmitz from *First Things* suggests that the deal even violates resolutions made at Vatican II, that the Church should support neutral religious liberties rather than seek privileges from the state. In other words, Francis won't jeopardize his progressive activism to protect children from being raped, but he *will* suspend those principles—along with centuries of Church tradition—to make deals with murderous totalitarian communists. Since at least as far back as Gregory VII, whose conflicts with Henry IV over the Church's authority were largely settled in Rome's favor, the Vatican has fought to resist state interference in Church matters.

---

[94] https://www.wsj.com/articles/china-and-vatican-to-sign-landmark-deal-over-bishops-1536929831

[95] https://www.theaustralian.com.au/news/world/vaticanchina-deal-panders-to-atheist-regime/news-story/bf6b644bb64df6ae5de369 13e0b3a8f4

[96] http://catholicherald.co.uk/issues/sep-21st-2018/chinas-war-on-christianity/?platform=hootsuite

[97] http://www.asianews.it/news-en/Fr.-Ticozzi:-'The-Chinese-government-wants-absolute-control-over-the-Church'-44974.html

As a communist dictatorship, China is officially atheist, tolerating some religions while viciously persecuting others. There are about twelve million Chinese Catholics, but their worship is severely restricted. The government regularly tears down crosses, burns Bibles, and puts believers in concentration camps, where they are gently reminded, on pain of death, to be loyal to communism instead of God.[98] As many as 90,000 people may be detained in these "re-education" centers. In August 2018, a Catholic news agency said Chinese police had broken up two summer camps for children aged eight to ten, accusing the organizers of holding an "illegal" Christian event. In March 2018, the government used a crane to rip the last cross from the roof of an iconic Catholic Church in Henan province.[99] This is the regime to which Francis has handed control of bishop selection.

And the cardinal at the heart of this deal between the Chinese government and Pope Francis, traveling regularly to Beijing on the pope's behalf over the past two decades until an unfortunate recent indisposition? That would be Theodore McCarrick, who by 2005 had been to China seven times on Church business.[100] According to Archbishop Viganò, one of Francis's first acts as pope—just three months into his pontificate—had been to return McCarrick to active duty by dispatching him on official Church business to the People's Republic.[101] After re-ingratiating himself with the Chinese regime, and of course being billeted by the Chinese in seminaries, McCarrick dismissed warnings from Chinese

---

[98] https://www.express.co.uk/news/world/1018337/Christianity-persecution-china-news-international-christian-concern

[99] https://www.christianpost.com/news/chinese-priest-captures-footage-of-officials-tearing-down-church-crosses-221338/

[100] http://www.30giorni.it/articoli_id_9610_l3.htm

[101] https://www.americamagazine.org/faith/2018/08/29/mccarrick-kept-robust-public-presence-during-years-he-was-allegedly-sanctioned

bishops about state interference in worship.[102] In February 2018, in an interview with *Asia Times,* Pope Francis made no mention of religious freedom, preferring to lavish praise on the Chinese government instead, telling the world not to fear its rise.[103] Gregory VII is looking down on us and he's just *thrilled.*[104]

---

[102] http://www.ncregister.com/daily-news/sino-vatican-relations-will-the-long-road-to-reconciliation-endanger-chinas

[103] http://www.atimes.com/article/at-exclusive-pope-francis-urges-world-not-to-fear-chinas-rise//

[104] https://en.wikipedia.org/wiki/Investiture_Controversy

IV.
FEMINISM IS
SPIRITUAL CANCER

I t might seem, with all this moral turpitude, as though we have returned to the Middle Ages. But it's actually much worse than that. The Church's original whistleblower on sexual abuse, Peter Damian, was an Italian cardinal horrified at the scale of sexual immorality throughout the Church. He wrote to Pope Leo IX in 1049 about rampant sexual harassment, concubinage, and bishops who failed to enforce church discipline. Damian wrote to duchesses, popes,and others to agitate for reform, with some success. He was something like an eleventh century #MeToo organizer, without the smugness and hypocrisy. It's sometimes claimed that Leo IX did not listen to Damian, but this is not true. It's an anti-Catholic smear that originated in early twentieth-century scholarship, much of which was seeking to overturn traditional Church teaching on sodomy. The lie, widely read in revisionist history such as Derrick Bailey's *Homosexuality and the Western*

Christian Tradition, has endured, without much evidence to support it.[105] It's incontrovertible, for a start, that Leo IX did a lot more than Pope Francis: priests who had violated their oaths by having anal sex, or having sex with lots of different partners, were barred from re-entering the priesthood.[106]

Dyan Elliott of Northwestern University gave a lecture in 2015 in which she says that the medieval church's fear of scandal created a culture in which secret sin was preferable to public shame.[107] "The very gravity of sexual sins seemed to argue for their suppression," she claims, which amounted to "a tacit policy that took its toll on the most vulnerable members of Latin Christendom." Elliott is wrong about the Middle Ages—but she's right about the present day. While Damian and Leo IX tried to do something about the problem, the modern Church has buried its head in the sand, preferring, as Elliott puts it, secret sin to public shame.

Damian was a strong advocate for celibacy, which is often cited by leftists as the reason for sex scandals. But if celibacy were the problem, you'd expect medieval clergy, who paid no attention whatsoever to injunctions about celibacy, to have healthier sex lives. The reverse was true: problems in the eleventh century church mirror our own but were far more widespread. Bishops were immune from secular law and could compel priests into acts of sodomy for their own amusement.[108] Many kept live-in prostitutes, which, if it happens at all today, is restricted to a few bishops in Rome. The celibacy requirement made no difference because it was routinely

---

[105] Hoffman, *The Book of Gomorrah*, 56–66.

[106] https://www.firstthings.com/article/2018/11/peter-damians-counsel

[107] http://cenhum.artsci.wustl.edu/events/04092015/Dyan-Elliott-medieval-church-pedophilia

[108] https://www.americamagazine.org/issue/534/article/11th-century-scandal

ignored—and men were not only getting married, but also practicing sodomy with underage boys, and other horrors. This suggests that the problem isn't celibacy, but men: give us an inch and we will take a mile. The only logical remedy is stricter enforcement of clerical rules for those who choose the priesthood as a vocation.

The reason the clergy should be celibate is that they serve God at the altar and not their own urges. It sounds extreme to modern ears, but Damian advocated for self-flagellation as one route to an intensification of the devotion to Christ. If that doesn't sound like fun, well, it isn't meant to be. The priesthood should be a calling, not a free lifetime membership to a gay bathhouse with the occasional pit stop to deliver a tedious lecture about diversity. Seminaries have been admitting trainees to the priesthood who are fundamentally spiritually unserious, and they should stop. It might be no bad thing for the priesthood to be thinned out a bit. After all, the problem is not a lack of priests. It's a lack of churchgoers produced by post-Vatican II vandalism. What brings people into the pews is serious devotion and the great drama of Christ's incarnation, crucifixion, and resurrection.

As Dennis Prager has pointed out, it was Judaism that first began the process of protecting and elevating women by putting the sexual genie in the marital bottle, ensuring that sex no longer dominated human interactions.[109] The Judeo-Christian tradition made it honorable to be the passive partner as a woman, elevating and celebrating womanhood as embodied by Mary in a way no other religious tradition ever has. Catholicism rejects the empty promises of the modern sexual revolution that have made both men and women so desperately unhappy. It forbids contraception as a violation

---

[109] https://www.nationalaffairs.com/public_interest/detail/homosexuality-the-bible-and-us-a-jewish-perspective

of the law of God and nature, while encouraging sexual pleasure between married couples.[110] Thanks to science we now know that birth control "makes women unattractive and crazy," as a handsome devil with a large campus following once put it.[111] The same guy also explained in some detail in December 2016 that the more we learn about our bodies and the universe, the more we realize the Catholic Church really is right about everything.[112]

An appreciation of the beauty and equality of the sexes heightened male-female love and sexuality, and made love and eroticism within marriage possible. Christian societies used the image of Mary to elevate women still higher, inventing consensual marriage and developing codes of chivalry, as we will see in a later chapter. But feminism reversed all this progress, telling women they were weak and in need of special protection from the horrors of men, and by characterizing the male, active partner's role as degrading and disreputable to women. Andrea Dworkin, one of the twentieth century's most influential feminists, said that women who have sex with men were "collaborators, more base than other collaborators have ever been: experiencing pleasure in their own inferiority." With the same upbeat optimism and lightness of touch we're used to seeing from Clintonian Twitter crazies, Dworkin insisted that "every woman's son is her potential betrayer and also the inevitable rapist or exploiter of another woman."[113] Over Dworkin's desk was a poster that read, "DEAD MEN DON'T RAPE." Dworkin, like

---

[110] https://www.breitbart.com/london/2014/12/04/the-sexodus-part-1-the-men-giving-up-on-women-and-checking-out-of-society/

[111] https://www.breitbart.com/tech/2015/12/08/birth-control-makes-women-unattractive-and-crazy/

[112] https://www.breitbart.com/milo/2016/12/15/full-text-merry-milo-christmas-minnesota-state-university/

[113] http://www.cathyyoung.net/bgcolumns/2005/dworkin.html

Arianna Huffington, married a gay man—though, unlike Huffington, she did so on purpose.[114]

Contrast this messy, miserable dystopia with a passage from Allan Bloom's last book, *Love and Friendship*, in which he talks about women's souls after Christianity: "Shakespeare seems to have thought that Christianity effected a deepening of women and a new sensitivity of men to them…the souls of women have become more interesting than they ever were, and Shakespeare is the poet of women at least as much as he is of men." And that's from a gay Jew who died of AIDS— not the sort of person you'd expect to speak fondly of the Catholic Church. But he's right, and the difference between the high pedestal upon which the Church places mothers and womanhood and the gutter the godless Dworkin sees herself occupying could not be more stark. God created Mary, the unspotted mirror who reflects his majesty, as a monument to his reverence for all women. As Fr. George Rutler puts it, feminists believe men and women are the same but unequal, while Christians know that men and women are equal, but not the same.

The best book on the feminization of the Church is Leon Podles' *The Church Impotent*, in which Podles explains in more detail than we can here just how the Church degenerated into its present unhappy state. While Islam and Judaism have predominantly male memberships, Podles notes, "Something is creating a barrier between Western Christianity and men."[115] Podles is scathing about the Church's cringeworthy attempt to "relate" to young boys by "comparing grace to jet aviation fuel." Podles leans heavily on one of the books that has made the most lasting impression on this author, David Gilmore's

---

[114] http://nymag.com/nymetro/news/people/features/11907/

[115] Leon J. Podles, *The Church Impotent: The Feminization of Christianity* (Spence, 1999), vii-xvii and *passim*.

Manhood in the Making. Go read it, and rejoin me here when you've devoured every line. It explains almost everything that has gone wrong between the sexes in Western civilization and which has in turn permitted the horrors of the #MeToo era and the farcical Brett Kavanaugh hearings to obtain.

The most damning observation about the Church that Podles makes is that it doesn't even seem to care that straight men are abandoning it. "Catholic circles are full of committees and conferences on the place of women in the Church, and almost none on the absence of men." In this respect, the Church is in sync with other left-wing institutions like the universities, in which women are flourishing, outpacing men, but at which only women's concerns are regarded as worth airtime and investment. The problem, as Podles explains, is especially bad in black churches, which are filled with misandrist women and which have nothing to say to disaffected young black men tempted into criminality and spiritual impoverishment. All that these left-wing Churches have to say about masculinity is that it is bad, it hurts women, men are properly the objects of fear, ridicule, and scorn, wherever possible male "toxicity" should be monitored, and boisterousness and overzealousness—critical components of healthy manhood—should be viciously punished. And what else should we really expect from an organization populated by tepid homosexuals and white-hot broads?

Gays flocked to the priesthood in the mid-twentieth century at the same time that some straight men were abandoning it. In the 1970s, hundreds of men per year left the clergy to get married.[116] The rise of feminism as industrial-strength man-repellant probably played some part in their initial decision-making. Don't underestimate how far men will run to get away from batty feminist broads—especially when they

---

[116] https://www.jstor.org/stable/1387312?seq=1#page_scan_tab_contents

get wind of how elegant and lovely are women of faith. For these men, the call of marriage and family, the cornerstone of the Catholic faith, was eventually too strong to resist. It must have been tempting in the mid-80s, during a feminist wave driven by obnoxious termagants, to escape to the seminary, a male-only safe space from which young men could simply check out of this cultural moment. Dworkin's 1986 novel *Ice and Fire*, capturing the spirit of the age, depicts every male character as cruel and repugnant, except one gentle soul—who is pleasant, because he is impotent. When that unfortunate condition is reversed towards the end of the novel, he too becomes a violent monster. *Ice and Fire* explains at agonizing length how sexual relations are by their nature a monstrous invasion of women, a theory that is an abhorrent inversion of God's intent. The narrator of her novel repeats the phrase "coitus is punishment," drawn from Kafka, throughout the book. This was a theme Dworkin expanded upon in non-fiction form with *Intercourse*. Apropos of nothing, Allen Ginsberg was an early mentor of Dworkin's, until she got annoyed by his relentless pursuit of underage boys.[117]

As the products of single motherhood—both gays and feminized men—have colonized the clergy, churchgoers have themselves statistically become more female.[118] This is likely in part a product of modern dysfunctional families, but, at least within the confines of church, it suits both groups. It might also explain the leftward lurch of so many Catholic dioceses in the Western world: gay priests and heavily female congregations. (And I do mean heavy. You should see some of the Church's most recent female recruits complain when they're told they only get one wafer each.) The idea of a sanc-

---

[117] https://www.feministes-radicales.org/wp-content/uploads/2010/11/Andrea-DWORKIN-Intercourse-1987.pdf
[118] http://padreperegrino.org/2018/08/24/ssapriest/

timonious social justice warrior in a chasuble banging on about diversity and global warming sounds ghastly to most of us, but to the disproportionately left-voting wives and mothers in the pews, perhaps it's just what the doctor ordered. Unfortunately, it's grotesque for the rest of us. Liberalizing churches has the well-documented effect of emptying them of worshipers, which is one reason Mass attendance has been flat under Francis, despite his supposed runaway popularity.[119] And it's men who are fleeing.

Just as you don't solve cratering church attendance by adding *more* of the thing that's driving it, you can't save the Church by throwing out the thing people come for: the rule book. Mainstream critics of Catholicism want it to modernize, by which they mean, "become more like us." More like NBC, we ask, which sent orders down from the "very highest levels" to stop Ronan Farrow's reporting on Harvey Weinstein? More like the academy, with its kangaroo courts and moral panics? Or more like New York governor Andrew Cuomo, who directed the state attorney general to halt its investigation into Weinstein six days after receiving a massive campaign contribution from Harvey's former law firm?

Those examples are drawn from a column by David French in *National Review*, which makes this observation: "Sexual libertinism has not created sexual utopia. Instead, it has created (as it always creates) a ravenous culture of sexual entitlement, exploitation, and abuse. Why do I feel the need to make this obvious point? Because there are apparently still people who believe that the path through Christian sex scandals—such as the abuse scandal that is rocking the Catholic Church—is the transformation and liberalizing of traditional Christian teaching about sex.... The path to scandal is indul-

---

[119] https://www.vox.com/the-big-idea/2017/7/14/15959682/evangelical-mainline-voting-patterns-trump

gence. The path through scandal is repentance. And the path to renewal is obedience. Distraught Christians shouldn't look to the world for inspiration. It has nothing to offer but the very misery we presently endure."[120]

It is easy to point to the transitory, sinful pleasures of the world, harder to make the argument for virtue. But calling people to worship *is* calling them to joy—to sing before the throne of the Lord in praise of His great work of creation. Living in sin is living in misery and shame, as the America of 2018, drenched in sexual permissiveness and racial animus, knows all too well. It shouldn't be as hard a sell as the Catholic priests are making it, which suggests that an alarming number of the Catholic priesthood simply aren't themselves conversant with the joy of being made in the likeness and image of our creator. They are too busy violating little boys, and have forgotten that their calling, while demanding, is a calling to joy. Too often, Catholic priests are not taking their service at the altar seriously, perhaps because their first experience was of a Church taking itself unseriously by not enforcing its own rules about homosexuality and celibacy in the clergy.

Despite everything we know about the deep dysfunction embedded in the curia, it's still the world that's broken, not the Church. The American institutions most completely sacrificed to the cultural left are the most broken of all, with colleges no longer capable of executing their core function, a media crippled by Trump-hatred and uncomprehending of half the country it presumes to report on, and an entertainment business imploding under the weight of harassment claims from hypocritical women…and that's before Hollywood's final reckoning, still on the horizon, when the

---

[120] https://www.nationalreview.com/2018/08/catholic-church-scandals-sexual-libertinism/

drink and drug-soaked exploitation of vulnerable young gay men and the systematic rape of children, both as endemic to Beverly Hills as child abuse is to the Catholic Church, finally come to light.

Beneath changing demographics in the clergy lies a more fundamental shift in the way the Catholic Church has operated and presented itself over the past one hundred years. Conservatives sometimes refer to it as the feminization or homosexualization of the Church, through progressive waves of left-wing entryism and aesthetic vandalism, aimed at the sort of sexual liberation French correctly warns will undo the Church from the bottom up if it is allowed to continue. Channeling the excessive energy of boyhood into a responsible masculinity is an essential rite of passage, without which a young man is doomed to a life of poor impulse control, dependence, and failure. The Church has completely removed itself from this critical moment in a boy's development, because it has become a place utterly unappealing to masculinity and outright hostile to heterosexual men—especially if they're conservative, and in the clergy.

Sometimes the assaults on Church traditions have come from within, such as the liberalizing ecumenical council Vatican II, which relaxed many of the rules on, for instance, the use of Latin in Church services. Post-Vatican II, priests were encouraged to face the congregation during Mass to make it more accessible, and discouraged from wearing elaborate vestments. The shocking state of contemporary Catholic music is a product of the "democratizing" effects of Vatican II, and something conservatives speak about today with sadness and horror. Progressive reformers don't restrict their entreaties to agreements made at the Second Vatican Council, but refer instead to the "Spirit of Vatican II" as carte-blanche justification for ever-more liberal approaches to liturgy and worship. Sound familiar? It should. It's what "living Constitutionalists" in the United States do when they don't like one of the rules.

One factor in the abuse crisis might be the priests reared in the strict Jansenist atmosphere of early twentieth century seminaries who were then abruptly shoved into an unduly permissive post-Vatican II world. It was the worst of all combinations, like delivering free beer and condoms to the teenagers in a strict Muslim household. Because liturgical changes as profound as Vatican II would have affected everyone in the Church, we shouldn't discount the possibility that the young men of the priesthood simply weren't ready for that much sexual and creative freedom. It's worth remembering that prior to Vatican II, at the start of the twentieth century, the priesthood was held in extraordinarily high regard.[121]

Vatican II absolved Jews past and present for the death of Christ and gave fresh weight and authority to the College of Bishops, but it also introduced indifference to some of the most precious customs and beliefs of the Church.[122] It's no mystery why so many young Catholics *adored* Benedict XVI's old-fashioned approach. But vanishingly few priests could tell you why. What passes for spiritual nourishment these days in too many Catholic parishes is the equivalent of empty calories from a candy bar: momentarily titillating on the lips, but not a bit satisfying or nutritious, serving only to enlarge the appetite for more empty things, and to make the nibbler fat. Crummy music, hideous vestments, and lectures

---

[121] https://www.catholicculture.org/culture/library/view.cfm?recnum=5915

[122] So hostile to the consequences of Vatican II are some traditionalist Catholics that there is even a movement called sedevacantism, which holds that every Pope since Pius XII is illegitimate because the mainstream church has embraced the heresy of modernism. Sedevacantists hold that the Holy See is therefore technically vacant to this day, and that there is currently no legitimate sitting Pope. I am free, and available to start work immediately.

about feminism. I'm not kidding! No wonder women love this new version of the Church, which consists too much of coasting on a surfeit of sugary emotional self-indulgence.

You feel great listening to one of these hippy-dippy sermons about recycling, or how it would be better if we all shared more with each other, or about how mean men are and how we should all be nicer to black people. Everything from Catholic priests these days is oh-so-nice and touchy-feely. (*Very* touchy-feely, if the moms aren't watching their charges carefully.) Nowhere to be found are the strict spiritual admonitions that the faithful, adrift in a disorientating, globalized world of hyper-consumerism, desperately crave. As Archbishop Chaput expresses it: "The big atheist murder-ideologies are dead. But they've been replaced by the far more effective practical atheism of a system based on consumer wants and needs. American advertising and entertainment are the most powerful catechists in history. Also, the most pervasive."[123]

The Church needs to wrest back that mantle. Rod Dreher's experience decades ago, of a Church that asks nothing of its followers and merely congratulates them for being who they already are, is not unusual.[124] And it has been getting worse. Nowhere to be found any longer are the masculine virtues of strength, courage, forbearance. Grit and gumption have become dirty words. As Robert Louis Stevenson put it, "Our religions and our moralities have been trimmed to flatter us, till they are all emasculate and sentimentalized, and only

---

[123] http://archphila.org/remarks-of-archbishop-charles-j-chaput-o-f-m-cap-at-the-faith-and-reason-institute-at-gonzaga-university-the-love-that-moves-the-sun/

[124] http://ideas.time.com/2013/09/29/im-still-not-going-back-to-the-catholic-church/

please and weaken. Truth is of tougher strain. In the harsh face of life, faith can read a bracing gospel."

Gone from the modern Catholic Church of Cormac Murphy O'Connor and Pope Francis is anything resembling manly fortitude. Willa Cather, most famous for her novels of the rugged frontier, never married but nonetheless appreciated the ineradicable need for manliness. She wrote:

> It makes one exceedingly weary to hear people object to football because it is brutal. Of course it is brutal. So is Homer brutal, and Tolstoi; that is, they all alike appeal to the crude savage instincts of men. We have not outgrown all our old animal instincts yet, heaven grant we never shall! The moment that, as a nation, we lose brute force, or an admiration for brute force, from that moment poetry and art are forever dead among us, and we will have nothing but grammar and mathematics left. The only way poetry can ever reach one is through one's brute instincts...A good football game is an epic, it rouses the oldest part of us, the part that fought ages back down in the Troad with "Man-slaying Hector" and "Swift-footed Achilles."[125]

Gone, too, from today's Church is the fire of righteous anger that believers feel when they see injustice in the world but for which their church provides no useful outlet. With its gay clergy and its estrogen-filled pews, it's not a stretch to say that the Catholic Church has become a pretty unwel-

---

[125] http://www.catholicherald.co.uk/issues/sep-14th-2018/the-wonderful-dread-of-american-football/

come place for masculinity and men in general. Even among the gays it's all limp-wristed leftism. The one good bit of gay culture—the worship of the hypermasculine—is missing entirely. I'm sure there is some ambitious young seminarian out there at this very moment planning a homily about "toxic masculinity" with which to impress his rickety old socialist bishop. How I wish I were joking: *America* magazine has already jumped on that bandwagon, which means the priesthood will shortly follow.[126] The social justice doctrine of toxic masculinity holds, following Dworkin, that all men are guilty of *something* and that widespread miscarriages of justice are therefore tolerable. But here's a question: to whom in the Church today does the young (heterosexual!) Catholic athlete or soldier aspire? If you can't answer, then, yup, we have a problem.

The make-up of the clergy—by which I don't mean the shade of foundation your local monsignor slaps on before hurling himself at seventeen-year-olds—does not reflect the congregation. It is too gay. We are constantly being told that politicians and actors on television should be more "representative," which is the Left's code for "anything but white." But there's no reason not to praise some degree of representativeness in principle, and especially from religious leaders. Which means we need more straight priests. If for no other reason than to correct the glaring deficiency of heterosexuals in the priesthood, the Church's ban on gay clergy should stay. You know, in the name of diversity and representation. That's normally enough to start a new episcopal initiative.

---

[126] https://www.americamagazine.org/faith/2018/09/19/brett-kavanaugh-and-toxic-masculinity-lessons-another-all-male-jesuit-high-school

V.
MAKE THE VATICAN STRAIGHT AGAIN

If you've made it this far, congratulations! You have a strong stomach. By now you probably have an image in your mind of a gay Catholic mafia secretly pulling the strings at the Vatican, with pedophile priests and other gay predators covering for one another and working overtime to smear their accusers and political opponents. Yup. That's pretty much what's been happening. Whether it's elderly antiques dealers and librarians cooing over elaborate vestments, arch-conservative British dandies rapturously describing the virtues of the Extraordinary Form, or sticky fingers at midnight in the seminary, Rome has been a haven for homosexuals, often with depressingly messed-up sexual attitudes and appetites.[127]

---

[127] http://www.slate.com/blogs/outward/2017/04/20/how_the_catholic_priesthood_became_a_haven_for_many_gay_men.html

Estimates place the percentage of gay Roman Catholic clergy anywhere between 15 percent and 50 percent.[128] An estimate from the 1980s placed the figure at 30 percent, with only half the clergy maintaining celibacy.[129] At the same time, Catholic priests have been found in a number of studies to be particularly well-adjusted, socially responsible, and interpersonally sensitive.[130] Men who join the priesthood generally report themselves being happy with their choice.[131] Perhaps that's because they have forbidden but satisfying sex lives. (They may well have sexually satisfying sex lives in part *because* they are forbidden—but that's a topic for a different book.) But at what cost to the health of the Church, and to the rest of us comes the priesthood's continuous post-coital bliss? Leon Podles writes that "perhaps it is the wounded who especially know their need for the healing touch of Jesus," which explains much of the present crisis and maybe also the Church's human resources catastrophe.[132]

Nothing has more clearly illuminated the Catholic clergy's descent into brutish, disheveled moral decrepitude than a recent news story about two podgy Chicago priests caught noshing one another off in the front seat of a car on a dirty weekend in Miami.[133] The more you delve into this story, as *First Things* editor Matthew Schmitz has, the worse it gets. Schmitz discovered that one of the priests was a graduate of a vocational men's program called Casa Jesús, which brought

---

[128] http://articles.latimes.com/2002/oct/20/local/me-gaypriest20

[129] http://usatoday30.usatoday.com/news/nation/2002/04/25/gay-catholics.htm

[130] https://link.springer.com/article/10.1007/s11089-005-6185-7

[131] Andrew M Greeley, *Priests: A Calling in Crisis* (Chicago: The University of Chicago Press, 2004), 58–59.

[132] Podles, *The Church Impotent*

[133] https://miami.cbslocal.com/2018/09/04/priests-arrested-miami-beach-sex-acts-in-car/

gay men from Latin America to Chicago. Casa Jesús was shut down over reports of a "depraved sexual culture." Journalists discovered that the program director had been in possession of child porn.[134] Another priest linked to Casa Jesús had been arrested in 2015, also on child porn charges.

Schmitz concluded, "What we see here is by now a familiar pattern: sexual criminality emerging in a context where non-criminal violations of clerical celibacy have become commonplace." This is an absolutely critical observation. It isn't any one sin—say, homosexual acts—that matter to the general trajectory of the Church as much as the toleration of sin in general. Let one in, and the rest will follow. Places where the Church looks the other way and tolerates wrongdoing, especially in its own house, are destined to become cesspools of vice, because that is how people work. It's the blind eye shown to gay sex that makes room for worse things to grow, especially among the gay men who know they will be given a pass and know there will be other gay men to stick up for them should they find themselves in trouble. Monsters are attracted to places where they know they can get away with murder, so obviously a homosexual person with depraved tendencies is going to latch on to a profession where illicit forms of gay sexual activity are systematically hushed up. The Church has practically hung a sign outside its door that says, "PERVERT WANTED FOR CUSHY PASTORAL ROLE, NO QUESTIONS ASKED!"

In this book we have wafted over the worst details of clerical child abuse, but you can read about them in excruciating, sick-making detail in Leon Podles's *Sacrilege: Sexual Abuse in the Catholic Church*, a book so graphic—necessarily so—that the publisher which originally commissioned

---

[134] https://twitter.com/matthewschmitz/status/1037044821553283072

it ultimately declined to publish the book.[135] I won't quote from it here, because I don't want to put you off. We're only halfway through the story, after all. But to fully grasp the enormity of the abuses and the monstrousness of those the Church has protected, Podles's book is unmatched in its level of detail. When the author sent copies out to his friends and contacts upon publication in 2008, abuse victims wrote to him in the dozens to thank him, but not a single priest dared to acknowledge the book's existence, presumably for fear of reprisals from their bishops.[136]

It's too easy to write the Catholic Church off as morally disordered, unhealthily obsessed with sex, or simply structurally corrupt and protective of powerful, abusive men. Historically, when national governments have persecuted, castrated, and even murdered homosexuals, the Church has not only shown them compassion but provided a route to a fruitful life in service of the community as members of the priesthood. There are easier ways of finding fresh meat to satisfy your sexual urges than spending seven years in penury training to become a Catholic priest. There appears to be a sweet spot in societies that stigmatize homosexuality that has led a lot of gay men into seminaries at various points in history. But those societies also have to be somewhat Catholic-friendly for it to be a draw.

The priesthood has been a home for sex offenders, including child predators. But it is worth bearing in mind the difference between priests found guilty of sex with a minor and what we might call full-blown pedophiles. Sometimes gays and pedophiles are the same people: although gay people are no more likely to be pedophiles, pedophiles are dis-

---

[135] Leon J. Podles, *Sacrilege: Sexual Abuse in the Catholic Church* (Crossland, 2008)

[136] Per Podles, in correspondence with this author

proportionately gay, although you're not supposed to say so out loud, because it upsets the gay lobby and politically-correct psychologists.[137,138] In any case, as often as a harrowing story about child rape emerges, there are a dozen or more about homosexual encounters in which the lines of consent are slightly less clear.

The majority of offenses involving priests concern youths below the age of sexual consent, with 51 percent between the ages of eleven and fourteen and 27 percent between the ages of fifteen and seventeen, according to the John Jay report, which was commissioned to determine the "nature and scope" of sexual abuse by Catholic priests in America between 1950 and 2002.[139] 80 percent of victims of clerical sexual abuse in a 2011 Philadelphia survey were identified as male teens or young men.[140] In an earlier study published in 2004, 87.4 percent were post-pubescent, with only a small number of allegations related to the abuse of children. The exploitation of these older teen boys is vile, illegal, an abuse of power, and may amount to rape, but it is not the same thing as pedophilia.

When a middle-aged priest is charged with statutory rape for having sex with a boy of seventeen who was a willing participant, we perhaps should not call that "child abuse," nor forget that the age of consent can vary even between Western countries. What is illegal in a northern state in the U.S. might not be in Germany, or even in a southern state of the

---

[137] https://www.researchgate.net/publication/12339526_Fraternal_Birth_Order_and_Sexual_Orientation_in_Pedophiles

[138] https://www.ncbi.nlm.nih.gov/pubmed/1556756

[139] http://www.usccb.org/issues-and-action/child-and-youth-protection/upload/The-Nature-and-Scope-of-Sexual-Abuse-of-Minors-by-Catholic-Priests-and-Deacons-in-the-United-States-1950-2002.pdf

[140] https://www.hprweb.com/2012/08/clergy-sexual-abuse-questions-remain/

union. And sexual mores change across time. The Spartans regarded gay pederasty as a fact of life, something we rightly find unsettling now.

Our neat line between "gay" and "straight" is a recent, man-made distinction. And it was only in the nineteenth century that "homosexual" began to appear as a definition of acts of sodomy and as a psychiatric phenomenon.[141] Modern psychologists believe that "homosexual" isn't a natural category of person: it's a construct, which means it can be un-invented. The Church, of course, was hundreds of years ahead of science, as it always is, by sharply defining the sinful dimension of homosexuality as the act, not the urge. We can love the sinner, who is powerless to control what he desires but can choose not to indulge. Scripture does not condemn homosexuals as a class of person; it condemns the act of sodomy.[142]

The latest research and the Church seem to agree—as do many gay conversion therapists—that a reduced preoccupation with "disordered" identities and a renewed focus instead on acts, the products of free will, given to us by Christ, is more faithful to how human beings actually work and more effective medical and spiritual therapy. Codifying someone as a "gay Christian" is theologically and psychologically illiterate, and presents the subject with a foreclosed identity that intensifies physical cravings and complicates his moral journey, reducing that person's complex whole to a single sin. It cuts off the road back from a sexuality formed out of social necessity, or in error.[143]

---

[141] https://www.firstthings.com/article/2014/03/against-heterosexuality
[142] Leviticus 20:13, 18:22
[143] https://www.breitbart.com/london/2015/04/14/im-sooo-bored-of-being-gay/

A clue to the Church's prescience on this is the low rank sins of the flesh command in the general taxonomy of wickedness, mentioned earlier. As ever, the compassionate and wise Benedict XVI got it just right. Writing as Cardinal Ratzinger in 1986, he cautioned against allowing characteristics such as sexual identity to represent the whole of a person, because it distracts from his fundamental identity as a creature of God.

> The human person, made in the image and likeness of God, can hardly be adequately described by a reductionist reference to his or her sexual orientation. Everyone living on the face of the earth has personal problems and difficulties, but challenges to growth, strengths, talents, and gifts as well. Today, the Church provides a badly needed context for the care of the human person when she refuses to consider the person as a "heterosexual" or a "homosexual" and insists that every person has a fundamental Identity: the creature of God, and by grace, his child and heir to eternal life. [144]

A traditional Christian teleology of sexual identity places marriage and procreation at the heart of everything we do as sexual beings. On this reading, gay men may be forgiven sexual transgressions if they also fulfil their obligations to the succeeding generations in some way, though this line of argument is used to excuse gay indiscretions in what is otherwise supposed to be a chaste clergy. What gay men should probably do is stay away from pastoral roles in the Church and find some arrangement through which they can have children,

---

[144] http://www.vatican.va/roman_curia/congregations/cfaith/documents/ rc_con_cfaith_doc_19861001_homosexual-persons_en.html

provided those children are reared in a stable home environment with both mother and father regularly present.[145]

(Children raised by same-sex "parents" fare poorly later in life, with more emotional problems than other children.[146,147] They are also more likely to turn out gay themselves, despite what left-wing activists claim.[148] The data suggest that under no circumstances should children be abandoned to be raised by lesbians. Lesbian domestic arrangements are routinely overshadowed by the ever-present threat of violence.[149] You would be better off taking your chances setting a wicker basket adrift in the Nile and hoping your tot gets plucked out of the water by the daughter of a wealthy family. I have written in the past about why gay men should "get back in the closet," somewhat satirically, but a version of the 1950s model, minus the queer-bashing, might be the best option for pious gay men wrestling with their options.[150] Let's face it, it couldn't be any worse than "Gay Pride.")

The numbers say that the vast majority of abuse cases do not involve young children. Philip Jenkins, professor of history and religious studies at Penn State and the author of *Pedophiles and Priests: Anatomy of a Contemporary Crisis*, wrote a widely-cited article for the *Pittsburgh Post-Gazette* in March 2002, titled, "The Myth of the Pedophile Priest." Jenkins shared data from the Catholic Archdiocese of Chicago

---

[145] https://www.breitbart.com/london/2015/05/07/kids-need-a-mum-and-a-dad/

[146] https://www.cbsnews.com/news/kids-of-gay-parents-fare-worse-study-finds-but-draws-fire-from-experts/

[147] https://papers.ssrn.com/sol3/papers.cfm?abstract_id=2500537

[148] https://borngay.procon.org/view.answers.php?questionID=000028

[149] https://www.breitbart.com/london/2015/05/07/attack-of-the-killer-dykes/

[150] https://www.breitbart.com/big-government/2015/06/17/gay-rights-have-made-us-dumber-its-time-to-get-back-in-the-closet/

that suggest a dramatically lower incidence of sex offenses than many readers might expect, and a huge drop from the heyday of abuse in the 1960s, '70s, and '80s. Outside the period between 1965 and 1980, when abuses peaked, much of the sexual abuse crisis in the Church boils down to quasi-consensual acts between older homosexuals and a mixture of straight and gay younger men who did not feel able to fend off advances at the time or speak about their experiences until much later.

Using a generous preponderance of the evidence standard, data from Chicago suggested that out of 2,200 ordained individuals only forty, or 1.8 percent, were probably guilty of misconduct with minors at some point in their careers. Out of that 2,200 there was only one pedophile.[151] Additionally, there is reason to suppose that the United States may be an aberration when it comes to clerical sexual abuse: data cited by Cardinal Vincent Nichols suggest a sex offender rate of just 0.4 percent of priests in England and Wales, a percentage that is accepted even by the Church's critics.[152] On the other hand, a full 7 percent of Australia's priests are said to have abused children.[153]

Not even priests themselves can agree on the causes of sex scandals in the church. In a 2002 survey, priests who described themselves as left-leaning said the key factor in the child abuse crisis is the requirement that priests be celibate, while self-described conservatives blamed it on homosexuals in the clergy.[154] Psychologists say neither is relevant to the

---

[151] https://zenit.org/articles/the-myth-of-the-pedophile-priest/

[152] https://www.firstthings.com/web-exclusives/2018/08/lessons-from-england

[153] https://www.cnn.com/2017/02/06/asia/australia-catholic-sex-abuse/index.html

[154] http://articles.latimes.com/2002/oct/20/local/me-gaypriest20

sexual abuse of children. Only a third of respondents claimed they "do not waver" from the vow of celibacy. The Church has never asked priests about their sexual orientation, though the official position is that homosexuals are barred from applying to become priests.

"Barred" might be a bit strong, since every time this position is clarified by the Church, "There follows a plethora of articles—including some in [Vatican daily newspaper] *L'Osservatore Romano* itself—in which the writers fall all over themselves to make sure that we understand that there must be (undoubtedly frequent) exceptions to every rule."[155] What becomes clear when you look at who is abusing whom is that this isn't primarily a pedophile problem: it's a gay problem.[156] (Incidentally, churches that ordain priestesses have experienced a similar phenomenon, only with lesbians, which suggests that the male-on-male dimension to the Catholic crisis may in part be a function of male-only clergy, and that the most instructive dimension of the crisis is indeed its homosexual nature.[157]) As Jeff Mirus of CatholicCulture.org writes, "Most Catholics would rather not have to think and speak endlessly about gay men, but the composition of their clergy leaves them with little choice."[158] I'm afraid he's right.

Given that the majority of encounters we are concerned with occur between priests and younger men but not children, we should focus not so much on what attracts perverts to the Catholic Church as we should a more readily explicable phenomenon: why the Church is so gay. Straight Catholics have been complaining for decades about tight-knit circles

---

[155] https://www.catholicculture.org/commentary/articles.cfm?id=753

[156] https://www.catholicculture.org/commentary/articles.cfm?id=752

[157] https://www.thetimes.co.uk/article/lesbian-priest-who-could-split-the-anglican-church-ttjtz6plwcr

[158] https://www.catholicculture.org/commentary/articles.cfm?id=460

of gay priests who cover for one another and punish anyone who calls out their misdeeds. Heterosexual whistleblowers are sometimes fired by their gay superiors.[159] This almost certainly has implications for the abuse crisis, in which powerful homosexual bishops hold the threat of termination above young seminarians' heads, which is only the second-worst thing they like to dangle in that position.

There are, by the way—and I should stress this is just my own observation—quite distinctively, *politically different* types of homosexuals in the Catholic Church. Some are the conservatives I alluded to earlier, who at least offer their charges a good glass of red wine, and perhaps an educational evening at the opera, before an awkward encounter back at the rectory. As I used to say about Fr. Michael, "At least he took a girl out for dinner first." These conservatives tend, in my experience, to fall into the category of inexperienced, quiet loner or repressed, sexually-bashful older gentleman. Many of the homosexuals in the Church are, in fact, liturgically and doctrinally conservative.

But then there are the more cliquey left-wingers, ruddy-faced, grinning, and usually corpulent, who run circles around their conservative counterparts in both technique and volume. These men are more likely to have well-connected friends and to seek power in the church hierarchy that will protect them. They're the Weinsteins and McCarricks of the Church world: more physically demanding and abusive, more sociopathic, more psychiatrically disturbed, always on the way from lunch with a high-ranking bishop or on the way back from an influential committee and, for all these reasons, to my mind, a lot more dangerous. For some reason, these are the priests who talk the least about God and

---

[159] http://www.flashreport.org/blog/2018/08/16/the-unsavory-rot-uncovered-in-catholic-dioceses/

the Bible and the most about climate change. I couldn't tell you why. What should concern us most about the Lavender Mafia isn't the fact that these priests are gay. It's that they use homosexual acts as an excuse, an outlet and a way to maintain power over others, and that they seem to be fundamentally immoral people.

McCarrick and others like him are lawless men, who think nothing of violating norms and rules if they can get away with it. They may well also be godless, even if they "believe they believe."[160] There is some awareness within the Church that the dilution of doctrine might be at the root of its present crisis. Cardinal Müller, who held the same top job at the Congregation for the Doctrine of the Faith as Joseph Ratzinger did, recently gave a strongly-worded speech in Rome insisting that a breakdown in respect for Church teaching and "rejection of the truth" is what has lubricated the way for depravity and scandal, and not "clericalism," the favored, nebulous excuse from Team Francis for moral failures.[161] "Evil acts must be condemned by ecclesiastical authority, the perpetrators punished according to law," said Müller. "With the idea that Christian dogma is no longer the ground and criterion of morality and pastoral care, a christological heresy comes into view."

The Lavender Mafia's homosexuality is related to what the Church regards as immorality, but probably only in the sense that gay people are more likely to have high I.Q. and thus belong to a category of people who habitually violate societal

---

[160] https://www.thecatholicthing.org/2018/09/16/when-the-priest-turns-atheist/

[161] https://www.catholicworldreport.com/2018/09/19/cardinal-muller-corruption-of-doctrine-always-brings-with-it-the-corruption-of-morals/

and evolutionary norms.[162] The precise relationship is not yet known, but studies consistently show a correlation between gayness and high intelligence.[163] Theodore McCarrick speaks five languages. Generally, researchers in the area believe that homosexual tendencies and intelligence are to some degree, perhaps mostly, inherited, though there is some reason to believe lesbianism operates differently.[164] (One theory holds that an allele controlling attractiveness *to men*, specifically, may be more pronounced in some individuals, which has the evolutionary advantage of encouraging a woman to have more children, while also producing male homosexuality as an evolutionarily insignificant byproduct.[165])

Behavioral scientists have suggested that high-I.Q. individuals "transcending" their evolutionary programming may perform an evolutionary function.[166] This could explain the disproportionate numbers of homosexuals in the arts and in other fields where breaking taboos is an advantage.[167] Upbringing is critical to how these genetic predispositions express themselves. McCarrick, for instance, grew up without a male role model after his father died when he was three years old.

But whether these experimenters and creative thinkers are the people we want in charge of religious institutions is highly questionable. High intelligence is a handicap in many professions. We don't need our bishops to be freewheeling intellec-

---

[162] https://calgaryqueerhistory.ca/2013/07/18/gay-men-are-smarter-than-straight-men-so-says-history/

[163] http://blogs.discovermagazine.com/neuroskeptic/2012/04/11/homosexuals-are-smart/#.W6AQkJNKiw5

[164] https://www.bbc.com/news/magazine-26089486

[165] https://www.bbc.com/news/magazine-26089486

[166] https://www.ncbi.nlm.nih.gov/pubmed/22293319

[167] https://www.breitbart.com/big-government/2015/06/17/gay-rights-have-made-us-dumber-its-time-to-get-back-in-the-closet/

tuals, anxious to experiment with their sexuality—and with the liturgy. We need them to be reliable moral compasses. We don't need DMV employees or TSA screeners running churches—just imagine sitting through their homilies—but neither do we need literary theorists or theoretical physicists.

It seems to me that the preponderance of homosexuals in the clergy is the result of faulty admissions criteria: the Church has been testing for intelligence, scholarliness, and cultural sophistication, welcoming all the eccentricity and peculiarity that goes with what is essentially now an academic body. Indeed—and this won't shock you—faculty members of American universities are disproportionately likely to be gay, even controlling for their political orientation.[168] Scoring seminary applicants highly for intelligence and sensitivity to art and culture is guaranteed to produce a heavily gay cohort. Other qualities make for better bishops, and should be reprioritized.

The homosexualization of the priesthood and the wider Church is one manifestation of a general weakening of religious institutions and of the faith generally, in part thanks to the communist infections of the 1930s and thereafter, and also thanks to the leftward drift of all major institutions in the West over the last century. But there's a more practical reason gays in particular didn't swarm the priesthood before 1900: in the 1800s, joining the clergy was no joke. Old-school Jesuit and Franciscan missionaries could expect to be in constant physical pain. Bishops, too, were badasses, as a long blog post on the subject of gay priests by Fr. David Nix in Denver explains:

---

[168] https://www.insidehighered.com/news/2016/01/26/study-suggests-faculty-members-are-disproportionately-likely-be-gay

Catholicism grows very well in pain and opposition. But by the time John F. Kennedy was President of the United States, Catholics were no longer sidelined, but rather mainstream. Fighting side-by-side with Protestants in two World Wars earned us the respect as equals [...] Catholics (and especially priests and bishops) went from unpopular and poor in the 19th century to popular and rich after the second World War. It came to be that if you want to live in a million-dollar rectory just for offering one Mass a day but you don't want to tell your mother why you don't like women, then the Catholic priesthood might be right for you!

As the padre puts it, with the switch from fringe belief to mainstream religion, Catholicism became a more convenient lifestyle choice for gays who might not want to hurl themselves into feats of physical endurance.[169] I don't know for sure, but I'm willing to bet the vast majority of gay priests are receivers—I mean they take it in the ass—and are therefore more fragile in constitution. They're the camp gays. Don't underestimate the effect of that on the Church as a whole. I certainly can't imagine many of today's frocked and perfumed monsignors signing up to get stung by scorpions on the walk from central Mexico to southern California, as St. Junipero Serra did. For too many priests—and too many female churchgoers, I suspect—religion has become a means of escape from the harsh realities of life, rather than a demanding, but ultimately rewarding, roadmap to spiritual liberation via the Via Crucis, or Way of the Cross.

---

[169] http://padreperegrino.org/2018/08/24/ssapriest/

At the core of Team Francis's immorality is not their sexual preference or even a crisis of faith. Rather, the Lavender Mafia are scheming, smart men who think the rules do not apply to them, and who have found a home with the occasionally naïve foot-soldiers of the Catholic Church, from whose citadels of power they can run amok. They resemble the corrupt, hypocritical regimes that dominate Hollywood, the academy, and the media—all, not coincidentally, places where cultural Marxism rules supreme. In a sense, the clerical abuse crisis in the Catholic Church is just another example of a rich, well-insulated, elite left-wing Establishment consumed by coitus, corruption, and cover-up. These people appear not to believe in anything at all except the pursuit of power—and boys.

It's no coincidence that the media run cover for Francis & Co., when so many of its own people use precisely the same mechanisms of control. This is why conservatives, sniffing a rat but not fully understanding the architecture of the media-academy-Hollywood-religion conglomerate, talk vaguely but angrily about left-wing gay mafias running the show and protecting each other. Such claims are typically sneered at by the mainstream, but they are correct more often than they are wrong.

Theodore McCarrick doesn't care much for the tenets of his faith, if his words and actions are anything to go by. But there is one religion he's fond of. Can you guess which one? In 2015, McCarrick addressed the Islamic Society of North America's interfaith conference in Virginia, calling the organization an "extraordinary instrument of understanding, instrument of cooperation, and instrument of beauty." In case that name doesn't ring a bell, ISNA was an unindicted co-conspirator in 2007's watershed terror financing trial, thanks to its deep links to the Muslim Brotherhood terrorist group Hamas.[170]

McCarrick unctuously praised ISNA's leaders as "so much a part of America and the *ummah* [that] is growing." He described ISNA as "very important to me," telling listeners that "the things that you believe are very beautiful." The guffaws from ISNA members after McCarrick left the building have sadly not been preserved for us. McCarrick was a regular flatterer of some of the most militant elements of Islam. He supported Georgetown University's Saudi-funded Center for Muslim-Christian Understanding, where he mingled with Islamic apologists and promoted Islamic propaganda films. McCarrick has been affiliated with several projects led by Sheikh Abdullah bin Bayyah, who has praised jihadists fighting Israel and the United States. McCarrick described bin Bayyah as "the prophet of light and the prophet of reason."

He isn't the only one. Much of the Catholic hierarchy has pandered to Islam. With the exception of Benedict XVI, popes have, for generations, appealed to Muslims for no discernible reason, while Muslims persecute and murder Christians all over the Middle East. They murder gays, too, of course—which ought to trouble the Catholic clergy more than it does, for obvious reasons. Back in 1999, John Paul II was proudly photographed kissing the Koran, a book that denies Christ. Why? Has any Muslim ever kissed a crucifix? If Catholic bishops spent as much time talking about sin as they do working out how to (pointlessly) reach out to Muslims, their congregations would grow fivefold.

---

[170] https://www.jihadwatch.org/2018/09/disgraced-cardinal-praised-isna-and-true-islam

VI.
MAKE WAY FOR THE IRRELIGIOUS RIGHT

What happens if we don't save the Catholic Church, and Christianity as a whole begins to wither and die? For one thing, the identity politics that plague modern life will never be beaten. The loss of religion in public life is what opened up the space for all these race hucksters and feminist dingbats in the first place. We are accustomed to the ugly, divisive strategies deployed by the political Left, and the effects of splitting us all up into distinct groups—gays, blacks, women. It isn't making for a happy or harmonious polity. But as bad as the Left's race-baiting and bullying of Christian bakers and endless hand-wringing can be, just imagine what will happen if the Right finally gives in, setting aside faith and universal moral principles and committing itself to the same ugly, identity-based conflicts. Is there a better way to win?

Yes, but doubling down on a secularized, technocratic "quest for truth" and leaning on classical liberal ideals aren't going to be enough to reverse the damage done to the West by cultural Marxism and the progressive Left. Jonathan Haidt, co-author of *The Coddling of the American Mind* and leader of the Heterodox Academy, is regarded as a leader in the pushback against political correctness on campuses. But, as Aaron Sibarium notes in his review of that book for *The American Interest*, Haidt isn't a threat to the Left, because he fundamentally misunderstands its nature and has failed to grasp the psychological implications of safe spaces and trigger warnings, which are a manifestation of "spiritual dissatisfaction," not "imperial ambition."[171] In other words, student insanity isn't a product of psychiatric dysfunction or fragility, but rather the product of ideology that has been brewing on campuses for decades. You can't fix the problem without purging the poisonous ideas that created it: identifying God-hating cultural Marxism as such, and beating it to a bloody pulp. Because it lacks a commitment to universal truths, value-neutral classical liberalism just "perpetuates the moral vacuum in which PC-culture arose." Likewise, the Church's current crisis is theological: too many of its bishops appear not to believe in God at all, or are at least very relaxed about setting aside Church doctrine when it suits them.[172]

Haidt and co-author Greg Lukianoff repeatedly object to left-wing absurdities as harmful to students, but not by explaining *why they are wrong*, which they cannot do without committing themselves to moral principles they think will alienate the non-existent reasonable middle they seek to

---

[171] https://www.the-american-interest.com/2018/09/19/the-bulverizing-of-the-american-mind/

[172] https://www.thecatholicthing.org/2018/09/21/doctrine-precedes-morality/

persuade. As Brigitte Gabriele once so memorably explained, "the peaceful majority are irrelevant."[173] Conflicts for the souls of civilizations are not won by gently taking the majority with you. They are won by pulverizing the extremes of your opposition into submission with relentless, aggressive, public displays of ritual humiliation and factual rebuttal. Haidt is probably capable of this, but, like everyone else claiming to lead the charge on campuses these days, he foolishly refuses to deploy the only strategies with any hope of success against the cultural Left. He and his Heterodox Academy are well-meaning, but completely ineffective. It will be left to the faithful to take up arms instead. I'd much prefer to see this battle played out in speeches and books and not on the streets, but not everyone shares my restraint.

Conservatives and especially Christians seem to have a natural aversion to political violence, which explains why there is such little right-wing violence despite decades of gruesome provocation, and outright violent attacks from Soros-funded groups like Refuse Fascism, commonly referred to as Antifa and identified by several agencies as domestic terrorists. Thus far, violent racism on the Right in America has been restricted to a small, unpleasant minority calling themselves the "alt-right," who have been endlessly covered by the media and hyped up into a scary rising force, but who in reality comprise a few thousand misguided nitwits. What happens, though, when the Right finally concedes to the Left's constant demands to treat race and gender as the pre-eminent defining characteristics of the self? Race war, obviously. And the whites will win. There are already groups of men out there in America preparing for just this kind of conflict, such as the Wolves of Vinland, a "Norse neopagan" men's society

---

[173] https://www.youtube.com/watch?v=Ry3NzkAOo3s

based in Lynchburg, Virginia. But there are still those of us who believe it would be better to avoid the conflict, if we can.

The Wolves of Vinland resemble a biker gang, except that its well-groomed, muscular members draw their iconography from Norse mythology and luxuriate in white power and white nationalist philosophy. The Wolves spend the weekends hunting, cooking, and eating their spoils and wrestling one another, which admittedly sounds titillating. But the world the Wolves of Vinland want to build is not one your gay, interracially-married author wants to live in. Should you happen upon their rippling torsos on a long walk through the Virginia woodland, I recommend *not* pointing out to these Norse fetishists that the Viking phenomenon might have been, at least in part, a product of the Islamic caliphate's need for slaves. Many Vikings in the east were slavers for Muslim overlords, and they only stopped selling their fellow man when—yup, you guessed it—they converted to Christianity. Ever wondered why progressive culture admires the brutal Vikings, glamorizing them in *Vikings, True Blood,* and *The Last Kingdom,* but demonizes the chaste Crusaders as lepers, crooks, and thieves in *Kingdom of Heaven?* The Vikings were pagans, and the Crusaders were Christians. Hence, also, the valorization of the Norse in Marvel's *Avengers* and *Thor* movies.

You should probably also avoid quoting the following, from New York priest and television host Fr. Rutler, unless you can render it in runes for them on a tree, and then run away quickly: "The increase in brutishness in our society parallels a decline in manly virtue. Enough realize this to have started groups that hold conferences and retreats to promote male bonding; but the model is a neurotic imitation of some Ostrogoth out in the woods making loud sounds with his body. The noble man must again arise, the manly father of the household and the manly priest at the altar, for masculinity is a sacramental of the paternity of grace."[174]

It's not just kooky masculinity cults in heavily forested, Washington, D.C.-adjacent states that spring up when you remove God from conservative politics. Take Richard Spencer, a white nationalist upon whom the left-wing press has lavished praise, describing him as "dapper" and "charismatic."[175] Spencer and I are often, absurdly, compared to one another, either through cluelessness or malevolence, but we could not be more different in basic philosophical outlook, to say nothing of his gauche dress and droopy bitch tits. Among the many deep ideological differences I have with Spencer, perhaps the greatest—greater, even, than our disagreements on race—is the fact that he is an atheist, and, consequently, pro-abortion.[176]

Revoltingly, Spencer says that one reason he is pro-abortion is that terminations are disproportionately performed on black babies. I'd normally chuckle at the sheer grotesqueness of such a statement, which ought to appeal to my twisted sense of humor. But it's the strangest thing. Abortion is the one subject on which even Milo Yiannopoulos is reflexively serious. I have to remind myself it's okay to crack jokes about it! If there's anything in the world that I am genuinely offended by, it might be the Left rebranding the murder of the innocent unborn as a "choice" a woman can make about her "reproductive rights." I find it viscerally upsetting, and for all my insight into the millennial social justice warrior's

---

[174] George William Rutler, "The Fatherhood of God," in *A Crisis of Saints* (San Francisco: Ignatius Press, 1995)

[175] https://www.dangerous.com/33029/10-journalists-in-the-mainstream-media-who-have-given-neo-nazi-richard-spencer-a-platform/

[176] https://www.theatlantic.com/magazine/archive/2017/06/his-kampf/524505/

unique pathology, this is one corner of the left-wing mind I don't think I'll ever truly comprehend. Perhaps it's my Catholic upbringing at work. Abortion and infanticide were approved of even by noble pagans like Aristotle. Banning them was one of the first things about the Catholic Church that really shocked the world.

The only young organization I've come across that gets the balance almost right is Gavin McInnes's boisterous and defiant Proud Boys, of which I am a member. Attendees at Proud Boy meetups, a mixture of ethnicities and sexual orientations, are united by their fondness for the unapologetic candor of Donald Trump, their hatred of feminism and political correctness, and their horror at the systematic undermining of the Western world by its own corrupted institutions. One of the fraternal society's mottos is, "I refuse to apologize for creating the modern world." Members describe themselves as "Western chauvinists." This is a step in the right direction. There are Christian members in leadership positions, such as Rufio Panman, famously caught on camera socking it to an Antifa protester.[177] But while explicitly non-racist, in general the group and its members do not prioritize faith over capitalism or democracy, which leaves space for a Christian brotherhood that can deliver on a religious revival that is the only plausible path to victory over the progressive Left. Naturally, because they represent a powerful counterweight and disincentive to the progressive Left's violent foot-soldiers, the Proud Boys are smeared by the media as "far-right," which appears in 2018 to mean "believes in the U.S. constitution."[178]

---

[177] http://officialproudboys.com/proud-boy-of-the-week/proud-boy-week-rufio-panman/
[178] http://www.latimes.com/local/california/la-live-updates-berkeley-ann-coulter-conservative-and-alt-right-groups-1493319826-htmlstory.html

The Left in America is famously and proudly godless. But do they really want this sort of irreligious Right? The Left has produced no effective antidote to Richard Spencer. He has not been humiliated in debate or driven from the dialogue. In fact, the Left has fluffed him up as evidence of an outpouring of white nationalism, while no-platforming me, because they consider a gifted and persuasive center-right personality a lot more threatening. America is showing itself depressingly incapable of resisting identity politics, because social justice has so deftly maneuvered itself into the space formerly occupied by God. A survey conducted by the Cato Institute showed that more religious Trump voters cared less about their skin color, while a quarter of those voters who had never been to church in their lives described their whiteness as a "very important" component of their identity. Among regular churchgoers the figure was just 9 percent, which suggests that white churchgoing Republicans might be the *least* racially motivated voters in the country. But this will not last forever.

It feels like a given in 2018 that "good works" are done by the state or by left-wing campaigners in journalism, the academy, and the entertainment business. Certainly, these are the people who crow most loudly about their own moral virtue. But this wasn't always so. Dorothy Day, whose political activism began in women's suffrage and who later became the twentieth century's best-known left-of-center Catholic, hated government welfare programs and railed against statism. She also, just to further warm readers to her, questioned America's endless foreign military entanglements.[179]

The Left is on the verge of squandering its moral authority with the public at large after giving in to its own crazy

---

[179] Nancy L. Roberts, *Dorothy Day and the Catholic Worker* (New York: SUNY Press, 1984), 164.

fringe. By actively preaching communism, as the New York-based journalists at social justice blog *Splinter* do every day, overly accommodating the race-baiters of Black Lives Matter and joining in the public ritual humiliation of Christian business owners, the media have alienated half the public already. Their sheer stupidity and cruelty will alienate the rest within another decade. Already, sensible people on both sides of the political divide pay no attention to journalists pontificating about race—especially those who have conjured up the imaginary boogeyman of white supremacy, which only exists to the extent that the Left itself has created it. The answer to all of this is God.

The power of fear-based public shaming is coming to an end, as the Trump election demonstrates. Ever-more Americans are defiantly standing up for what they know to be a superior form of social organization to the oppressive cultural Marxism of the Left: capitalist Christian democracies are the best way we've come up with so far to organize large groups of human beings to live together in relative harmony, which is why I like to tell my college audiences that America, with its historically enthusiastic embrace of capitalism, Christianity, and democracy, is the greatest country in the history of human civilization.[180] What few on the political Right have grasped is that the most important component in this trifecta isn't capitalism, or even democracy, but Christianity.

Conservative commentators like the *Times*'s Ross Douthat do not appear to have much faith in the power of Christ to recover from Christianity's apparent decline in the West and the current scandals.[181] But what actually happens when the

---

[180] https://www.breitbart.com/milo/2016/10/16/milo-us-lesson-islam/
[181] https://www.nytimes.com/2018/09/15/opinion/sunday/conservatism-after-christianity.html

political Right finally says okay to the Left's provocations? As someone who has reported on the far-right in America—and been blackballed by the journalistic establishment for daring to give them a fair hearing—trust me when I say the results will not be pretty. With religion driven from the public square, race will become the prime motivating force behind political action. What will a newly race-conscious, mostly white, heavily-armed, routinely censored Right think of the media's constant and unfathomably stupid white-bashing? They will view it, of course, as an assault on their identity, requiring a forceful and violent response. The first shoots of this are showing themselves already. Progressives who say the election of Donald Trump was a cry of anguish from white America aren't entirely wrong—but the Left is uncharacteristically coy about who created such a relentlessly hostile atmosphere for ordinary, God-fearing, working-class white Americans that they took the drastic step of electing a faintly ridiculous reality TV star to the country's highest office.

Yet the Trump presidency is nothing compared to what's coming if the Left can't break its addiction to mocking straight white males.[182] If the reputation and practice of Christianity in the West can't be restored, along with a healthier regard for the masculine virtues, America is at risk of sliding into pre-medieval tribalism. You can't expect innocent, working-class straight white men, who are told from birth that the value of a person is rooted in his skin color, sexuality, and gender and that everyone should be *extremely and very loudly proud* of things they had no control over, *unless* they are straight, white, and male, in which case *you are a cancer to society and deserve to be punished and publicly humiliated even though you didn't personally do anything wrong*, to endure the

---

[182] https://www.avoiceformen.com/featured/in-praise-of-dead-white-men/

injustice and indignity for long. As I say, sooner or later you really might kickstart an armed white pride movement.

Remove God from the conversation and you don't magically gift society with a public square that operates on elevated Enlightenment principles of reason, logic, and nice manners. All you do is make room for evil to take His place, whether race war, gender animosity, obsessions with gay and transgender rights, or bizarre preoccupations with the civil rights of illegal immigrants, the most unhinged version of Marxism to express itself in the culture thus far. Unlike religion, which makes people healthier, happier, and more productive, these alternative routes to redemption leave individuals miserable and societies scarred by wars fought over imaginary grievances. This could all have been avoided in America if the Right had put up more of a fight when the Left ridiculed and bullied Christianity out of popular culture.

Maybe Catholics can lead the way in setting it right. It's a wonder to me that the response of working-class white Christian America to the indignities showered upon it by smug liberals has been so *mild*. Trump is the least that coastal left-wingers deserve after two generations of race-baiting. But responding to victimhood and special pleading with yet more identity politics isn't the answer. Nothing short of a full religious revival is required throughout the Western world if we are to avoid civil war. If you're reading this book, you might be one of the people who could kick it off. And that's why it's so crucial we protect or restore the institutions that bind us together, the most important of which is the Church.

There's an old joke whose original teller escapes me: if you were on the way home late at night and you heard footsteps behind you, would you be more or less concerned if you knew they belonged to someone coming from Bible Study? You don't have to be a Catholic, or even a Christian, to see that Judeo-Christian societies are fairer, happier, healthier, and more tolerant than others. If you're disabled, female, black, gay, or any other disadvantaged group you care to mention, there's nowhere better to be than in a rich Western liberal democracy whose society is underpinned by Judeo-Christian principles. Yet the progressive Left in America seems determined to tear down everything that has made the West a nice place to live for people who aren't rich straight white males.

Since 2004, the Institute for Studies of Religion at Baylor University has been producing reports that demonstrate how much safer and more pleasant western Christian societies are and providing evidence for the social and economic value of unfashionable organizations such as the Boy Scouts.[183] By demonstrating the specific and unusual greatness of Christian civilizations, the Institute consciously performs the role for the twenty-first century what atheist philosopher Ludwig Feuerbach unintentionally did in the nineteenth: teaching us the true character and utility of religion as a cohesive force in society and as an agent for social mobility, economic growth and, most of all, simple human kindness. The Institute's research proves how much Christianity fosters "prosocial behavior, family life, population health, economic development, and social conflict," and shows how religious-based rehabilitation programs have vastly better outcomes in prisons, especially for the most serious crimes, including violent offenses.[184]

The more you look at the numbers, the more you realize *Christianity just works*. That's because it satisfies an intense longing in the human soul that can't be fully sated by anything else. It can be softened by a profound love, though even those deeply head-over-heels for one another still cannot find everything they need in another human being. It can be

---

[183] http://www.baylorisr.org/publications/

[184] http://www.baylorisr.org/about-isr/mission/

transformed into something pleasurable, albeit ephemeral, with art and music. But only regular participation in public worship can really nail it for you. Study after study has shown that religious people are less anxious and less depressed than other people.[185,186] The more religious you are, the happier you get, the more time you spend with loved ones, and the more generous you are, according to Pew data.[187]

> Roughly two-thirds of highly religious adults (65 percent) say they have donated money, time, or goods to help the poor in the past week, compared with 41 percent who are less religious. And 40 percent of highly religious U.S. adults describe themselves as "very happy," compared with 29 percent of those who are less religious.

The single biggest factor in determining whether someone will be content with his life is, believe it or not, whether he regularly participates in public worship. That's why progressive social justice warriors love public shaming and Twitter mobs—it's their version of going to church. Modern progressivism shares many functions and rituals with organized religion, which is what makes it so powerful and so dangerous: it capitalizes on the innate human need for a higher power or greater purpose. The social justice version of Mass is a destructive caricature of the real thing, but it does make you feel better for a while, because one of the most powerful

---

[185] https://www.scopus.com/record/display.uri?eid=2-s2.0-84870705914&origin=inward&txGid=53d6bcc0b4db3dc0afc3b8efc4cae86e

[186] https://www.scopus.com/record/display.uri?eid=2-s2.0-17744393482&origin=inward&txGid=d72545cbf3ea3443ac91ef33d7407882

[187] http://www.pewforum.org/2016/04/12/religion-in-everyday-life/

psychological and emotional benefits of religion is a keener awareness of family and spiritual community. Catholicism makes this emphatic: the family, not the individual, is the fundamental unit of society.

Like capitalism, or the British monarchy, to the unbeliever Christianity might not make a lot of sense on paper. It's imperfect, for sure. But it works better than anything else, and better than some other, almost equally popular religions. Government data from the UK released in 2016 showed Muslims only very marginally happier than atheists.[188] Despite all these advantages, the Catholic Church is experiencing an unprecedented crisis in authority. That same Pew study discovered that three quarters of Catholics look to their own consciences for "a great deal" of guidance on difficult moral questions. Just 11 percent said they looked to the pope.

Both Left and Right, without religion, slide into totalitarianism. The yearning in the human heart to which Christianity speaks has been filled by many evil diversions throughout history. Social justice has filled the void in America, aided by the expulsion of Christianity from public life after decades of ridicule and marginalization by the ascendant cultural Left, starting in the 1960s, coincidentally just the time that abuse started taking off in the Church. The Nazis in their pomp and violence, and the social justice warriors in their righteous Twitter crusades, both reach for that same ecstasy felt by a nun in prayer, or by a churchgoer during Mass, or by any one of us in quiet contemplation of

---

[188] https://www.huffingtonpost.co.uk/2016/02/02/office-for-national-statistics-well-being-data_n_9138076.html?guccounter=1&guce_referrer_us=aHR0cHM6Ly93d3cuZ 29vZ2xlLmNvbS8&guce_referrer_cs=M-kUYCOCaUfU3cCkXGjJl2g

a great work of art. C.S. Lewis describes that yearning, and where it comes from, in *Mere Christianity*:

> If I find in myself a desire which no experience in this world can satisfy, the most probable explanation is that I was made for another world. If none of my earthly pleasures satisfy it, that does not prove that the universe is a fraud. Probably earthly pleasures were never meant to satisfy it, but only to arouse it, to suggest the real thing. If that is so, I must take care, on the one hand, never to despise, or to be unthankful for, these earthly blessings, and on the other, never to mistake them for the something else of which they are only a kind of copy, or echo, or mirage. I must keep alive in myself the desire for my true country, which I shall not find till after death; I must never let it get snowed under or turned aside; I must make it the main object of life to press on to that country and to help others to do the same.[189]

Evelyn Waugh was reaching for the same place in *Brideshead Revisited*. Passages like the following explain why the novel is so beloved by Catholics:

> [P]erhaps all our loves are merely hints and symbols; a hill of many invisible crests; doors that open as in a dream to reveal only a further stretch of carpet and another door; perhaps you and I are types and this sadness which sometimes falls between us springs from

---

[189] C.S. Lewis, *Mere Christianity* (1952)

disappointment in our search, each strain-
ing through and beyond the other, snatching
a glimpse now and then of the shadow which
turns the corner always a pace or two ahead of
us.[190]

Totalitarian ideologies such as Nazism and progressivism
offer false hope to those seeking to impose control on a disordered inner world. There is no salvation to be found in
getting a journalist fired for an off-color joke, just as there
was no redemption to be had at the barrel of a Luger in
Berlin in 1945. The dopamine hit from getting Alex Jones
banned from every social network must have felt good to
CNN media reporter Oliver Darcy, who had been aggressively lobbying Twitter, Google, and Facebook to nuke the
radio host from their platforms. But the following morning,
Darcy's still miserable, and he's still going to Hell.

The Left's journey to godlessness is almost wholly com-
plete with its embrace of social justice, identity politics, and
socialism. They may be lost to us, and we don't yet know what
Generation Z—which is intensely skeptical of religion while
at the same time supportive of traditional family structures
and dismissive of feminism—has in store. But we can start by
re-energizing ordinary people about their faith. It is the only
thing that will save our civilization—never mind our immortal souls. And even if you don't believe in all that, the extraordinary non-material benefits of prayer should be enough to
tempt you at least to try it out. What have you got to lose?

---

[190] Evelyn Waugh, *Brideshead Revisited* (1945)

VII.
THE POPE MUST DIE[191]

Catholics can be endearingly touchy about criticizing the pope. As they know, he's only "infallible" in a technical sense—at certain times, in certain circumstances, in published dogmatic statements that apply to the entire Church. (In fact, the doctrine of papal infallibility has only been explicitly invoked once, in reference Mary's Assumption, since it was defined by the first Vatican Council in 1870.) But to speak badly of *il papa* is bad form. Cool, whatever! These are not ordinary times. Francis is certainly not impeccable, which is what most people think is meant by infallibility. He is certainly capable of sin (*peccatum*). The question is: does he have enough years left in him for all the Hail Marys he's about to be given in the confessional?

---

[191] Ordinarily, a humorous reference to a 1991 comedy film starring Robbie Coltrane would not require further explanation, but, in these idiotic times, it may be necessary for me to clarify that I am not seriously calling for the assassination of Pope Francis. Indeed, my publisher insists on such a clarification. So here it is.

Typically, when picking their new papal name, popes choose the moniker of a previous pontiff they admire, or whose work they seek to emulate. Pope Francis picked an entirely new name, a move presumably calculated to signal his independence and lend verisimilitude to descriptions of him as a "maverick." How many future popes, one wonders, will pick the name Francis, eager to celebrate his legacy?

When Ross Douthat posed the question in the *Atlantic* in 2015, "Will Pope Francis Break The Church?" he wondered aloud whether conservative elements in the Church would react badly to the elevation of a pontiff named for the left-leaning, reformist *Vicar of Christ* in the iconic 1979 novel.[192] Douthat lavished praise on Francis, per the fashion of the age, in awe of the "attention-grabbing breaks with papal protocol, the interventions in global politics, the reopening of moral issues [and] the blend of public humility and skillful exploitation…of the papal office." Might Francis, Douthat asked, have the same transformative activist tendencies as that fictional hero?

Douthat, like others before him, tried to be cautious—he is a rare example of a writer in the public sphere who actually does know a thing or two about Christianity—but the effect of all this unusual praise and close attention was to create an entirely fictional version of Pope Francis, one that existed only in journalists' imaginations, that of a cerebral, globalist pontiff ready to welcome gays openly and satisfy progressive Catholic fantasies by never missing an opportunity to talk about "global inequality." It isn't hard to find otherwise sober news stories between 2014 and 2016 piling on the praise, such as a *Washington Post* story that breathlessly describes

---

[192] https://www.theatlantic.com/magazine/archive/2015/05/will-pope-francis-break-the-church/389516/

him as, "the freewheeling Argentine pope who loves gays, loves divorcees, and hates income inequality."[193]

What the facts of Jorge Mario Bergoglio's life show is something quite different: intellectual sloppiness, ruthless careerism, and a lifelong dedication to ambiguous public statements that hide shifting political positions and a lust for power. For someone who apparently loathes Donald Trump, Francis shares many of the U.S. President's more grating qualities, including a lack of intellectual seriousness and a lifelong addiction to praise. Unlike his predecessors Benedict and John Paul, he has none of the real estate mogul's affable public persona—or weird, counterintuitive likeability. As for his dreary sermons on income inequality, this is a pope who freely admits he doesn't have the slightest clue how the global economy works.[194]

The journalists who hated Benedict XVI—they weren't quite sure why, but they'd heard he was conservative, so they made every effort to pick sinister-looking photos and generally signal their disapproval—thought they were getting an Obama-style, hope-and-change pope in Francis. They didn't realize that he is better described as Clintonian, with a cult of personality that demands absolute obedience and loyalty. Above all else, Francis is a politician content to make some pretty shocking moral compromises to preserve his power. As reliable a guide to Francis as any of the ecclesiastical positions he may have held prior to being elected pope are the debts he has to the European cardinals who got him the job, including some of the most theologically left-wing men in

---

[193] https://www.washingtonpost.com/news/morning-mix/wp/2014/11/10/after-demotion-from-pope-francis-cardinal-raymond-burke-falls-from-vatican-grace/?utm_term=.4bb64e78e373

[194] https://www.nationalreview.com/corner/pope-admits-he-knows-nothing-about-economics/

the church, such as England's Cormac Murphy O'Connor and Germany's Walter Kasper.

You may remember Walter Kasper as the cardinal who was sent home almost the moment he landed in the UK with the pope in 2010, for referring to Britain as a "third-world country," apparently a reference to its multiculturalism. Typical of the progressive left-wing elite from which he hails, Walter Kasper is a snob, a racist, and a liar, but most importantly a hypocrite. He once denied that he snootily referred to the opinions of African church leaders with the word "taboo" and dismissed their views as unimportant—despite the fact that Africa is undoubtedly the future of the Catholic church, while in Kasper's native Germany, Catholicism is practically extinct. But Kasper had to confess that this denial was a lie after the release of a tape on which he said exactly what Vatican journalist Edward Pentin had reported.

The balance of power has shifted in the Church dramatically since Francis took office, with minor figures promoted because they have the right progressive outlook on things, and well-respected traditionalists and conservatives humiliatingly and, in at least one case, repeatedly demoted.[195] The electoral pact through which O'Connor, Kasper, Godfried Danneels, and Karl Lehmann formed "Team Francis" to get Bergoglio elected is explicitly forbidden by the apostolic constitution governing papal elections, but no one moved to stop them. Possibly, no one saw it coming. As I've alluded to already, I've been told by editors of Catholic magazines that there's a ferociously conservative, traditionalist revival happening among millennial Catholics that's at odds with the burbling emotional incontinence of the elderly left-wingers who currently run most archdioceses.

---

[195] https://www.usatoday.com/story/news/world/2014/11/08/pope-francis-demotes-conservative-us-cardinal-raymond-burke/18710769/

One of the most distressing things about the leftmost wing of the college of cardinals is how little they seem to reflect on God. These aging hippies have bought into the modern fad for all-consuming identity politics hook, line, and sinker—hence the Church's embrace of hardline left-wing social activism. But the cardinals seem not to realize or care that the progressive worldview they are pandering to punctures their own spiritual authority. The second that Francis was inaugurated, the four aging Team Francis cardinals set about machinating for aggressive liberalization of the church, for which pew-sitting Catholics have shown no enthusiasm at all. Even left-wing voters don't like the politically-correct excesses of the elites.[196] Liberalizing Christianity until it's basically indistinguishable from secular society is one of the factors in declining Church attendance, and *everyone knows this.*

Francis has even started to echo trendy critiques of the Church in his pronouncements on gay marriage and abortion. He has blessed lesbian authors of books about the virtues of gay parenting, despite evidence that children raised by lesbians suffer damaging psychological consequences and are much more likely to witness domestic violence in the home.[197, 198] He has cracked jokes about Catholic women "breeding like rabbits."[199] Perhaps his most cravenly atten-

[196] https://www.theatlantic.com/ideas/archive/2018/10/large-majorities-dislike-political-correctness/572581/

[197] https://www.breitbart.com/london/2015/05/07/kids-need-a-mum-and-a-dad/

[198] https://www.breitbart.com/london/2015/05/07/attack-of-the-killer-dykes/

[199] https://www.ncronline.org/news/vatican/dont-breed-rabbits-was-pope-francis-breaking-new-ground-birth-control

tion-seeking stunt was washing the feet of Muslim migrants, insisting, "we are all children of the same God."[200]

If I ever hear another bishop claiming that Muslims and Christians worship the same God I am going to vomit. Claiming Allah is the same as the Christian God, just worshiped in a different way, is a strategic lie. It's a set up so Muslims can describe Islam as the "perfected" version of Christianity and refer to "reverts" instead of "converts." Left-wingers take their word for it and say Jews, Christians, and Muslims are all "people of the Book," but we aren't, are we? Allah is an irrational, capricious tyrant who can make two plus two equal five at a moment's notice, not the source of love and rationality whom Catholics worship. Muslims do not believe in the Trinity and they deny the divinity of Christ. There's not much room for maneuver.

Have the doormats we call our spiritual leaders any idea how enthused the faithful would be to see them put Catholics first for once by telling the truth about this enduring but false claim? I should say that there are plenty of learned people, including Leon Podles, who say it's a bit more complicated than I'm suggesting. But even if the question of whether we worship the same deity is less clear-cut than I think it is, why do our popes and bishops behave like needy ex-girlfriends around imams who do not share their desire to reach across faith divides? Muslims do not seek interfaith understanding. They seek conquest.

Most disturbingly for conservatives, and most significantly for the future, Francis has sent signals that he wants divorced and remarried couples to receive communion, yet

---

[200] https://www.washingtonpost.com/news/worldviews/wp/2016/03/25/children-of-the-same-god-pope-francis-washes-the-feet-of-muslim-migrants/?utm_term=.2739cef5ee0e

another embrace of moral relativism.[201] The pope's defenders in the media describe this as "meeting people where they are."[202] Theodore McCarrick boasted in a speech in Boise, Idaho in 2014 of the assistance he had provided Pope Francis with this effort.[203] But watering down the rules about who can receive communion is the first step in tossing out centuries of Catholic moral teaching, with the end goal of abolishing the charge of adultery altogether. While ordinary Catholics crave moral guidance, and his priests desperately need a new, rigorous level of oversight, Francis gives speeches describing sex as "not a taboo" but rather a "gift from God," the clear implication of which, in line with his other recent statements, is that the Church should relax about matters of sexual behavior.[204]

Social justice-watchers from other fields know this playbook well: first, a minor change is slipped in under the rubric of "guidance," "terms of service," or "community guidelines." Then the change starts to be enforced ever more strictly. When it is accepted as settled, further concessions are demanded or slipped into new versions of the rulebook. This is how American universities fell, not through revolution, but with a thousand tiny concessions to progressive entreaties, all of them packaged in the language of forgiveness, tolerance, and love. Fast-forward a generation or two and everything the organization once stood for is essentially gone; all that remains is a vast, self-serving bureaucracy operated for the benefit of a clique of morally reprehensible people.

---

[201] https://www.crisismagazine.com/2018/amoris-laetitia-can-jeopardize-seal-confession

[202] https://www.americamagazine.org/faith/2016/04/08/top-10-takeaways-amoris-laetitia

[203] https://www.youtube.com/watch?v=XHWRDTcKVAY

[204] https://cruxnow.com/vatican/2018/09/18/pope-francis-says-sex-isnt-taboo-but-a-gift-from-god/

Like their progressive equivalents elsewhere, it seems Team Francis would rather rule unchallenged over a diminished and disgraced institution than wield influence in a strong, politically-diverse Church that reflects the concerns and priorities of ordinary Catholics and within which they might have to jostle for power. But the pursuit of power at all costs, lashed to a superficial commitment to left-wing social and economic causes, has led to moral horrors, with ruthless, opportunistic leaders commanding squadrons of bishops who believe that ushering in a Soros fever dream of open borders and "soak the rich" tax regimes is a higher priority than the immortal souls of their flock.

I'm exaggerating, but not by much. Team Francis has the same brazen, shameless, contemptuous attitude, holier-than-thou demeanor, and mind-blowing lack of perspective as the social justice warriors we're familiar with from social media. Take Francis's most loyal lieutenant in the United States, Blase Cupich, a cardinal who defended the pope's refusal to comment on the Viganò letter—I am not making this up—with the following words: "[T]he pope has a bigger agenda... he's got to get on with other things [such as] talking about the environment and protecting migrants." This is the sort of hot air that fills Catholic sermons in the West these days. Not a lot of talk about sin—unless it's Trump's—and rather a lot about environmentalism, globalism, socialism, and social justice. Don't be surprised if the next time your local priest takes to the ambo, he has more to say about white supremacy than salvation.

So absent is God from the modern Church that satire of the right-on preoccupations of Catholic priests has become prophetic. In August 2018, the *Babylon Bee*, a satire website, published the parody headline, "Pope Says He Will Address Sex Abuse Scandal Once He's Finished Talking

About Climate Change."[205] It was a mere two months before
Cupich provided something even better in real life. *Mirabile
dictu*, the social justice tendency in the College is concentrated among its most elderly members, who have been play-
ing a long game to get one of their own on the throne, which
at least offers them a little hope for the future. O'Connor's
generation will be dead soon, taking their emetic 1970s politics—and dress sense—with them. The '70s truly were "a
kidney stone of a decade," as Garry Trudeau once quipped,
and the Church needs to rid herself of the products of that
sorry decade as quickly as possible.

A few days after dismissing the Viganò letter as a dis-
traction from hand-wringing about migrants, and even when
the dreadful implications of the letter were becoming clear,
Cupich told a group of seminarians: "I feel very much at
peace at this moment. I am sleeping okay."[206] If you're getting
the impression that these guys can't possibly be real, that their
public statements are just too wildly tone deaf to be authentic,
that they must be fictional villains… well, you're not alone.
Even Catholics are getting sick of it all, musing aloud that
Francis is an "exceedingly uncertain trumpet." The author of
that phrase, Jeff Mirus, the founder of CatholicCulture.org,
characterized Francis's effect on the Church like this:

> A hard-won Catholic renewal is being
> dismissed in favor of focusing on those few
> Christian values which the world is still willing
> to tolerate. For the past fifty years, this has been

[205] https://babylonbee.com/news/pope-says-he-will-address-sex-abuse-scan-
dal-once-hes-finished-talking-about-climate-change/
[206] https://chicago.suntimes.com/news/blase-cupich-catholic-sex-abuse-
scandal-we-have-bigger-agenda-than-be-distracted-tells-mundelein-
seminarians/

a recipe for Catholic laxity and disintegration. It has also hastened the ascendency of a dominant secular culture which relegates Catholics (and other sincere Christians) to a second-class status, and that's putting it mildly.[207]

What none of us knew at the time Ross Douthat was writing his *Atlantic* story warning of a brewing schism in Catholicism was that Francis would indeed come close to breaking the Church. But it wouldn't be over politics, at least not directly. Instead, thanks to his inexcusable decision-making when rehabilitating political allies who had appalling abuse records, even going so far as to overturn the decisions of Benedict XVI to reinstate sex offenders and child abusers, Francis has distinguished himself not as the reforming moderate of Douthat's imagination, or the progressive hero of the media's, but instead as a grubby, corrupt friend to any left-wing cardinal who maybe buggers eleven-year-olds, sure, but can be relied upon to do the pope's bidding when it matters so, you know, let's give the guy his old job back, and refuse to answer any questions when his victims finally pluck up the courage to point fingers.

The Church must now take a proactive stand against abuse as part of a wider, more fundamental series of reforms. One idea, suggested by Matthew Schmitz, is for the Church to push for new laws, making it a civil crime for clergy to abuse those over the age of eighteen in addition to minors.[208] Schmitz is right that taking the initiative and pushing for these laws in states that do not have them would not only be properly penitential, but it might also help restore the

---

[207] https://www.catholicculture.org/commentary/articles.cfm?id=690
[208] https://www.wsj.com/articles/stopping-the-priests-who-prey-on-adults-1536879580?mod=e2tw

Church's stained reputation. The abuse of adults has been scrupulously ignored by Francis and the entire American Church, with "vulnerable adults" only very recently added to the list of victims whose abuse warrants punishment. That term refers only to adults with handicaps, mental and otherwise, so it wouldn't include the seminarians Uncle Ted McCarrick preyed upon. Sometimes, clergy engage in consensual sex with one another, but as part of the Church's necessary renewal, leaders should root this out almost as enthusiastically as they do the abusers of teenagers. Is Francis the right man to lead such a reform, tainted as he is by scandal and by his close alliance with Uncle Ted?

Although Benedict XVI as Pope Emeritus has become a symbol of the conservative resistance to Team Francis, it's not for his pastoral or leadership abilities. Rod Dreher, writing in the *American Conservative*, reminds us of a fifth-century student from Rome who would later become St. Benedict, who "withdrew from the city of Rome because it was so corrupt, and because he feared that if he stayed, he would lose his soul."[209] His namesake, the Pope Emeritus, is said to have had precisely the same experience. Benedict XVI is a gifted theologian and scholar, but not an especially talented leader. Friends say he realized he was powerless over the ingrained Vatican bureaucracy and the Lavender Mafia and that he was not well suited to fighting the "filth" he saw infecting the Church from root to branch. In more recent private letters, Benedict seems to express consternation at the present situation and regret that his name is mentioned at all, even by his supporters. He appears to want to disappear entirely.[210] So it

---

[209] https://www.theamericanconservative.com/dreher/joseph-ratzinger-benedict-option/

[210] https://www.miamiherald.com/news/nation-world/world/article2187
16265.html

isn't clear who might lead a purge of the corrupt old order. But we need someone, our own Donald Trump, to follow the failure of the "maverick" McCain—I mean, Francis. He must be somewhere. Probably not in the priesthood.

Fortunately, for now, the American laity is robust and independently-minded, tired of excuses and ready for new leadership, even if that is leadership further down the food chain, like, say, parish priests who adopt more of a "get on with it and apologize later" approach than has traditionally been considered the Catholic way, and who recognize that bishops have squandered their moral authority and that parishioners have basically had it with the Church hierarchy for a while, and just want to get back to worshiping God properly without all the left-wing moralizing, cover-ups, hypocrisy, rainbow-flag chasubles, and crappy acoustic guitar music.[211] And books condemning Francis are now being published at a quite remarkable rate.[212]

There are also feisty publications springing up like Church Militant, a website scrappy enough to alienate the snobs and doctrinally rigorous enough to be intimidating—both check marks for me. (Its critics call it the Catholic Breitbart, which they mean as an insult.) Francis can't eradicate the problem, because he's part of it. Instead, he continues to double down on the mistakes that created a lack of accountability in the Church the first place. The pope continues to strengthen the executive authority of the Rome-controlled synod of bishops, at the expense of good bishops who will be bullied into

---

[211] https://www.firstthings.com/article/2018/10/catholicism-after-2018

[212] Philip F. Lawler's *Lost Shepherd: How Pope Francis is Misleading His Flock* (Washington, DC: Gateway, 2018), not otherwise quoted here, is among them

accepting the latest nuttery from Team Francis.[213] Archbishop Chaput has publicly released a scathing critique of the synod's latest working document, which provides a basis for discussions the next time the synod met.[214] The synod is dedicated to young people, which, Chaput rightly suggested, is not an appropriate subject for such heavily compromised people to hold forth on. He also objected to theologically nonsensical concepts such as "transgender Catholic" appearing in Church documents.[215]

I can't pretend I didn't cheer when I read that a priest in Chicago had defied his local bishop and burned a gay rainbow flag that had been displayed in his church in an "exorcism ceremony."[216] It wasn't any ordinary pride flag, but a flag that blended the cross with the rainbow—a symbol, say parishioners, that the parish's former pastor, the notorious Fr. Daniel Montalbano, had earmarked it as the new "gay-friendly" Chicago parish after his previous church, St. Sebastian, home to gay Masses, had burned down. Montalbano, it is reported, was close friends with the leading left-wing Cardinal Joseph Bernardin, who presided over a Mass with a rainbow flag draped over the crucifix. Montalbano died aged fifty, found dead in the rectory bedroom in which he held gay sex parties. His body was discovered naked and hooked up to what

[213] http://www.ncregister.com/blog/edward-pentin/pope-francis-boosts-authority-of-the-synod-of-bishops

[214] https://www.lifesitenews.com/news/us-archbishop-raises-alarm-over-youth-synods-working-document f

[215] http://archphila.org/archbishop-chaputs-first-synod-intervention-at-the-synod-2018-on-young-people-the-faith-and-vocational-discernment-october-4-2018/

[216] https://www.nbcnews.com/feature/nbc-out/parishioners-defy-chicago-archdiocese-burn-rainbow-flag-exorcism-ceremony-n910666

journalists are coyly calling a "sex machine."[217] This was later covered up by Church officials.[218] The parish's new pastor, Fr. Kalchik, himself a victim of clerical sexual abuse, was protesting about the political statement the pride flag was making, especially in light of the gay sex scandal engulfing the Church.[219] Kalchik is the face of heroism in today's Church. He is one of the few priests prepared to stand up to the Lavender Mafia. What they've done to him in revenge beggars belief.

Fr. Kalchik had gone into hiding at the time of this writing, because his bishop—the aforementioned Cardinal Cupich—threatened him with forced psychiatric assessment and even hinted at his death.[220] Cardinal Cupich threatened to have him evicted by police if he did not attend St. Luke, a treatment center whose former CEO was convicted of embezzling $200,000 and spending the money on his gay lover.[221] Kalchik had previously written a letter to Francis, as a former victim, begging the pope to act more decisively against abusive priests and those who shelter them and speaking about Chicago's gay mafia.[222] Perhaps that marked him out for punishment: the two priests dispatched to discipline

---

[217] https://www.churchmilitant.com/news/article/chicago-vicars-threaten-priest-for-burning-rainbow-flag

[218] https://www.theamericanconservative.com/dreher/persecution-father-paul-kalchik-white-martyr/

[219] http://www.chicagotribune.com/news/local/breaking/ct-met-church-addresses-banner-burning-20180921-story.html

[220] https://dwightlongenecker.com/the-curious-case-of-fr-kalchik/

[221] https://www.churchmilitant.com/news/article/chicago-vicars-threaten-priest-for-burning-rainbow-flag

[222] https://www.churchmilitant.com/news/article/one-priests-plea-to-pope-francis

and threaten him for offending gay sensibilities were both known to be implicated in the Chicago wrongdoing.[223]

Cardinal Cupich may have no time for doctrinal fidelity, but he has been coached "for years" in far-left transgender ideology by a social justice warrior called Alexandra Whitney, who says she pressured him to ditch Kalchik.[224] There is now a petition circulating calling for Cupich to resign.[225] As Fr. Dwight Longenecker, a popular Catholic blogger, puts it: "So we have a priest who has been traumatized by gay sex abuse and who dissents from being steamrollered by the rainbow brigade? Fire him. Kick him out. Send him to the looney bin. Write him off. Throw him under the bus. Call the police."[226] Rod Dreher has correctly called Kalchik a "martyr."[227] Dreher also quotes an unnamed priest whose grimly fascinating letter is worth reprinting in full, about the sorts of malicious punishments that can be visited upon priests who step out of line with the politically-correct consensus:

> There is nothing that the laity can do to protect priests. Bishops have total authority over us. We can certainly walk away. We can leave. But Kalchick [sic] is a great example of what happens when a priest stands up to his bishop's agenda. He's probably done as a priest.

---

[223] https://dwightlongenecker.com/the-curious-case-of-fr-kalchik/

[224] https://twitter.com/iskandrah/status/1043800348383694848?ref_src=twsrc%5Etfw%7Ctwcamp%5Etweetembed%7Ctwterm%5E1043800348383694848&ref_url=https%3A%2F%2Fwww.theamericanconservative.com%2Fdreher%2Fpersecution-father-paul-kalchik-white-martyr%2F

[225] https://www.change.org/p/cardinal-cupich-must-resign

[226] https://dwightlongenecker.com/the-curious-case-of-fr-kalchik/

[227] https://www.theamericanconservative.com/dreher/persecution-father-paul-kalchik-white-martyr/

He can submit to St. Luke's and get the evaluation, but St. Luke's has an alliance with the bishops as well. It's the bishops who pay the bill. When a priest goes there the priest must sign a release for everything he discusses to be turned over to the bishop and the diocese. So how is he supposed to deal with any real psychological issues he might have knowing that the data is going to be sent back to the bishop and put into files or even potentially released or used against him? Point being, the priest isn't free. It's a coercive environment. It's rigged against priests and the information can be used by bishops to continue to manipulate those priests for years to come, all under the guise of "I just want Fr. X to be healthy." What they are really after is reconditioning priests to act within a particular safe metric to avoid bad publicity or cause problems. Sounds a bit Orwellian doesn't it?

Another side of this is that bishops have to hold liability insurance on their priests and if the priests have some kind of HR problem or Occupational Problem in their parish, the insurance companies are demanding bishops send them to places like St. Luke's for a kind of "reconditioning therapy" that they don't actually need. The priests are not actually in any kind of need of psychological assistance, but for the Diocese to continue to have them covered with liability insurance the insurance company puts pressure on the bishop for them to demonstrate that they have taken measures to lessen liability. A St. Luke's program of six months of incarceration and therapy with five years of outpatient programming is just such a program. All of this goes into the priest's file and is held against him the rest of his career to be trotted out any time he gets out of line.

Notice, none of this has to do with the abuse of children. Perhaps some with moral failure or bad decisions. Maybe decisions that would cause a layperson to lose their job. But in the priesthood, you get the shame of six months of incarceration in a lock-down facility and forced psychological treatment that even these facilities know you do not need. But they participate in the sham because it's big revenue and they are cashing in on the bishop's need to cover their liability. This is happening in large numbers throughout the country to priests.[228]

Expect to see a lot more Extraordinary Form Masses quietly appearing across Catholic America, as traditionalists get more of the sort of worship they want, whether their bishop likes it or not. The laity in the United States is a great deal more God-fearing than its clergy, more respectful of historical tradition, and less afraid than ever to announce itself, despite smirking and ridicule from the liberal establishment. There are a still a few rebellious, heroic junior priests like Fr. Kalchik eager to help them. And, for the first time in living memory, the laity seems prepared to turn its back on the current pope if that's what it takes to survive.

---

[228] https://www.theamericanconservative.com/dreher/persecution-father-paul-kalchik-white-martyr/

Francis has been described by those in the know as a "Peron-ist."[229] This basically means, "he won't go quietly."[230] In the manner of an abusive husband who threatens to abandon his bruised and bloodied wife should she dare to complain about her twice-weekly beatings, Francis threatens to quit when his feet are held to the fire: in May 2018, under pressure over cover-up allegations, he hinted that he might retire.[231] But there's no reason to suppose he will ever leave by choice. If he won't resign, he can't be forced out, so his critics have no choice but to wait for him to keel over or be persuaded that he is no longer the best man for the job. Conservatives are sticklers for the rules, and this is a big one. You can't force a pope out. There's no appetite for a coup, say those experts, which would return the Church to the bad old days of popes and anti-popes, during which there were competing claims of legitimacy from rival camps, each of whom said their man was the "real" pope. That sort of chaos really would tear the Church apart.

Conservatives worry that two popes resigning in a row would permanently change expectations of papal terms. Before Benedict it had been 600 years since a pope had resigned. If Francis were to go early as well, there would no longer be a presumption that new popes planned to die in office. Political opponents would then become incentivized to make popes miserable until they resigned. If cardinals know a pope can be pressured to give up his seat, pressure will be applied. This, too, could tear the Church apart, forever diminishing the standing of the Bishop of Rome. The papacy would become just like any other political appointment, subject to the same vulnerabilities and ugly clashes as any other sort of leadership. As the *Weekly Standard* terrifyingly prophesied: "Before you know it, you'd have polling data and opposition research."[232]

There are some quirky ideas floating around the blogosphere, such as whether Francis can be sued as a private individual for his role in covering up child abuse scandals.[233] But there appears to be no appetite for any strategies that would imperil future papacies, or further damage the office. His staunchest critics are wondering, therefore, if Francis can simply be endured. Sitting out the reign of a lame duck pope would resemble what Bob Woodward says is going on in the Trump White House: there's a guy in the chair issuing orders, but it's essentially up to his subordinates to decide whether or not to follow them. And information coming to the big desk is strictly limited. Popes eventually die, but the Church endures. Can the Church in her present condition survive that kind of entropy? Yes, but only if we embrace a paradoxical and unexpected route: a religious revival, and a call to arms for new converts and the de-fagging of the Bride of Christ. Now is the time to convert to Catholicism. Not to save a few corrupt old queers in purple robes in St. Peter's, but because we recognize "the nature of the Church, the truth of its foundation, sacraments, saints, and the real presence of Christ in the Eucharist."[234]

The Lavender Mafia may control the papacy, and even the Holy City, for now. But their reign will not last forever. We

---

[232] https://www.weeklystandard.com/jonathan-v-last/vigano-letter-mccarrick-wuerl-and-pope-francis-are-breaking-the-catholic-church

[233] https://rorate-caeli.blogspot.com/2018/08/downfall-not-so-hypothetical-legal.html

[234] https://pjmedia.com/faith/why-now-is-the-time-to-convert-to-catholicism/

cannot leave it up to the remaining sound bishops to wrest back power from these amoral careerists, who have sheltered pederasts and pedophiles for decades. It is time for ordinary Catholics to stand on their hind legs and roar, by withholding donations to organizations and agencies that do not do good Catholic work and by loudly, insistently demanding the resignations of anyone tainted by the present scandal and any future similar scandal, no matter how deeply or painfully that may cut into the college of cardinals, and with no regard paid to the politics of those involved. We embark upon this journey because no other future is conceivable, and because we know that only with legions of fresh blood can we effect the coming purge of corrupt cardinals and bishops and start our beloved Church on the path to redemption.

Scrubbing the effeminate, the weak, the dishonest, the disreputable, the duplicitous, and the malevolent from the Church will make way for the restoration we really need: a restoration of manhood and a strong Catholicism that recognizes the equal but different contributions of men and women and embodies the best of both of them. Manliness is what the Church is lacking. It's a willingness to expose yourself to enemy fire, whether it comes from critics on social media, gunfire on the battlefield or the horrors of the Passion. It is the impulse opposite to the sniveling cowardice of the petty palace intriguer. As Rod Dreher says, anyone who fails to teach young men the masculine God of scripture leaves young men vulnerable to the false gods of race and ideology, or—Dreher doesn't phrase it like this, obviously—leaves them to turn into low-testosterone soy-boys who blog about microaggressions for Buzzfeed. Whether or not you wear a uniform, you can still be manly and courageous in defense of family, church, country, and civilization. When Pope Francis puts on his uniform in the morning, for whom is he fighting?

There's a phrase from Chesterton I like that has become something like my personal motto: *laughter and war*. That works well for a mischievous culture warrior like me. But the full passage, from *Heretics*, is worth some reflection in the context of a Church that has lost its manhood and absorbed "a critical mass of morally depraved and psychologically defective clergymen who entered the service of Church seeking emoluments and advantages unrelated to her spiritual mission, in addition to leaders constitutionally unsuited to the exercise of the virtues of truthfulness and fortitude."[235]

> The Salvation Army's "methods are the methods of all intense and hearty religions; they are popular like all religion, military like all religion, public and sensational like all religion. They are not reverent any more than Roman Catholics are reverent, for reverence in the sad and delicate meaning of the term reverence is a thing only possible to infidels. That beautiful twilight you will find in Euripides, in Renan, in Matthew Arnold; but in men who believe you will not find it—you will find only laughter and war. A man cannot pay that kind of reverence to truth solid as marble; they can only be reverent towards a beautiful lie. And the Salvation Army, though their voice has broken out in a mean environment and an ugly shape, are really the old voice of glad and angry faith, hot as the riots of Dionysus, wild as the

---

[235] https://www.catholicculture.org/culture/library/view.cfm?recnum=5915

gargoyles of Catholicism, not to be mistaken for a philosophy."[236]

Good mental hygiene requires us to have the proper, natural response to things, whether good or bad. It is right and proper to hate hateful things. And we should not abandon outrage to the emotionally damaged twenty-somethings on Twitter. The political Left knows this, but wants to deny its enemies the same weaponry it has, which is why leftist activists are violent, hysterical, perpetually outraged crybabies who nonetheless require delicate handling so they don't fall apart. We should respond appropriately to such base manipulations, and refuse to play along. We should fight fire with hellfire. "Our national life is ended," write Lunn and Lean in their *Cult of Softness*, "as soon as it has lost the power of noble Anger. When it paints over and apologizes for its pitiful criminalities...dares not decide practically between good and evil, and can neither honor the one nor smite the other, but sneers at the good as if it were hidden evil, and consoles the evil with pious sympathy, the end is come."[237] Michael Brendan Dougherty, in an excellent summary of the crisis for *National Review*, says:

> Ultimately the vision Francis has promoted presents a God who is not merciful but indulgent, even lazy, and indifferent... He expects less of you, and you can expect less of Him. In this new religion, where our faults become semi-virtues, salvation itself is changed. Instead of a free gift from God, it becomes a

---

[236] G.K. Chesterton, *Heretics* (1905) https://www.gutenberg.org/files/470/470-h/470-h.htm

[237] Lunn and Lean, *Cult of Softness*

debt owed to us. Christ is not moved by an act of love to sacrifice himself as a propitiation for sinners. Instead, he dies on the cross because our human dignity, revealed in our semi-virtues, obliges him to do so.

What Francis is slowly instituting is a religion of presumption. A religion of "good enough," where our misguided efforts put God in our debt. Communion becomes a participation trophy. And by freeing the Church from its preoccupation with outdated sins such as adultery, Francis can refocus the Church on the things he likes to denounce, such as the building of border walls, or air conditioning.

And no wonder, then, that the Vatican itself is filled with moral mediocrities, with men who are sexually and financially compromised.[238]

"The ideology of masculinity," writes Leon Podles, "has replaced Christianity as the true religion of men."[239] What is needed now is a fusion of the two. Spiritual fatherhood—the deepest masculinity—is the only way out of the Church's present crisis. Sometimes that is going to mean *being angry*. "What's so black and white to most dads and moms is somehow, inexplicably complicated for some prelates...good spiritual dads not only don't abuse their children but become ferocious in protecting their children from those who try. They also justly become white hot furious whenever anyone hurts their kids or looks the other way."[240]

---

[238] https://www.nationalreview.com/magazine/2018/10/29/case-against-pope-francis-catholic-church/

[239] Podles, *The Church Impotent*

[240] http://www.ncregister.com/blog/fatherlandry/spiritual-paternity-anger-lying-and-vulnerable-adults

Yet too many priests in the modern Catholic Church keep strength and masculinity hidden, or apologize for it, because they have such a complex relationship with their own. Too many priests have no sense of moral responsibility for their charges. And just look what happens when men are sidelined from religious life and the Church's ministers give up on their primary function: women suffer too. Witness the west-coast maenads calling themselves as "witches," who define themselves by their "rage" and "axes [they've] got to grind."[241] This outpouring of Wiccan fetishism among Hillary Clinton devotees is another example of modern society devolving to the pre-medieval without the guiding light of Christianity. If there's one thing we know from Euripides—and *Buffy The Vampire Slayer*—about the old gods of paganism, it's that anyone who actually does meet the deity to whom they are offering goat entrails ends up insane or dead.

Men like Archbishop Chaput (whose lecture on "Why Men Matter" gave me hope that at least some priests get it) are in short supply.[242] It is not enough just to be nice—true faith requires a lot more of us than politeness.[243] Too often we're subjected to mawkish bullshit about acid rain or guns from weak duds like *America* magazine's James Martin, who never met a left-wing cause he didn't like, especially if it somehow undermines core Church teachings and provides an opportunity to wallow in helplessness and self-pity.[244] Sometimes a

---

[241] https://www.cnsnews.com/news/article/michael-w-chapman/witches-hex-justice-kavanaugh-occult-ritual-nyc?utm_source=sumome&utm_medium=facebook&utm_campaign=sumome_share

[242] http://archphila.org/archbishop-chaputs-address-at-salinas-mens-conference-why-men-matter/

[243] https://www.crisismagazine.com/2018/genuine-faith-requires-more-than-niceness

[244] https://www.americamagazine.org/faith/2017/10/02/sad-tired-and-angry-prayer-face-gun-violence

man must make a stand, and he must do so angrily and righteously. Pope Francis does not understand righteous anger, or he would never have rehabilitated Theodore McCarrick. "No wonder this church has a pope who refuses to wear red shoes. They symbolize martyrdom. That's for heroic Christians, not for men like Pope Francis," writes Dougherty. Perhaps that means Francis cannot lead the Church and its wild gargoyles. As the Rev. Jerry J. Pokorsky puts it:

> The sense of abandonment by the Holy Father is palpable. The most strident but provocatively honest comment I received was from a pastor serving in a diocese apart from mine: 'The Holy Father has left us orphans. He prefers to protect…buddies rather than His bride the Church (in direct opposition to Christ laying down his life for the Church). Francis is the ultimate symbol of the crisis of masculinity in the West. He is neither father nor husband.'[245]

Sadiq Khan, the Mayor of London, had conservatives frothing at the mouth when he suggested that a few acts of terrorism now and again were basically part and parcel of living in a big cosmopolitan city. I don't *think* he meant to make excuses for the terrorists' actions—though, since he is a man who merrily attends gender-segregated events to suck up to Muslims with regressive social attitudes, who knows? What I think he was getting at was that these occasional horrors were a price worth paying for multiculturalism. I don't agree, obviously, either that the horrors are occasional or that such

---

[245] https://www.thecatholicthing.org/2018/09/08/restoring-confidence-in-the-catholic-faith/

mindless multiculturalism is worth a damn thing. Khan is offering multiculturalism as a form of redemption—appeasement to the gods of diversity for colonial sins past, perhaps. I offer a lot lower risk, with much higher reward.

Although Khan's premises are faulty, his reasoning is sound. The world *is* messy and imperfect, inside and outside of the Christian. As the novelist Flannery O'Connor wrote to a Protestant friend who was considering the leap to Rome but was daunted by the Church's surface flaws:

> It is easy for a child to pick out the faults in a sermon on his way home from Church every Sunday. It is impossible for him to find out the hidden love that makes a man, in spite of his intellectual limitations, his neuroticism, his own lack of strength, give up his life to the service of God's people, however bumblingly he may go about it [...]
>
> You don't serve God by saying the Church is ineffective, I'll have none of it. Your pain at its lack of effectiveness is a sign of your nearness to God. We help overcome this lack of effectiveness simply by suffering on account of it. [...] To expect too much is to have a sentimental view of life, and this is a softness that ends in bitterness. Charity is hard and endures.[246]

If you're a Catholic devastated by what's happened to the Church in this "summer of shame," take heart.[247] The Church has survived five apocalypses already, including the Arian and

---

[246] Flannery O'Connor, *The Habit of Being* (New York: Farrar, Straus and Giroux, 1988), 307-8

[247] https://www.catholicworldreport.com/2018/09/20/the-sixth-death-of-the-church/

Albigensian heresies, Voltaire and Darwin. As Chesterton wrote, in a book that was crucial to C.S. Lewis's conversion, "Christianity has died many times and risen again, for it had a God who knew the way out of the grave."[248] No one besides children and Democrat voters believes that you can save everyone: there are always ugly moral compromises to be made. And so it is with the Catholic Church. The charges laid against her are vast and grave, and the Church is probably guilty, or at least guilty enough to warrant wholesale reform. But we would be insane to throw out the very basis of our civilization, welcoming in all manner of horrors, from Islam to the progressive Left, to occupy her place—just because the Church's ministers have gone astray.

As Fr. Rutler once observed, the real danger to society is not merely a lack of virtue. It's a lack of heroism. There is a generation of young men without proper moorings who could be molded into soldiers of Christ, filled with that glad and angry faith by the right spiritual leader. To save the West, we have to bring these men back to the Church. If men lose their bond to the Church, then the secular world, which will always be dominated by men, also loses its connection to the Church—and to her truths. Pope Francis does not speak to these young men, whose faith is kept alive in spite of his spiritual guidance, not because of it. Without discipline and leadership, my generation and the one after it could easily topple into barbarism. Look to the East, and consider the virility and malevolence of Islam. That's why a clerical purge is needed now. Not just because of the crimes and the cover-ups. Not because gays can't *ever* be good priests. But because the faithful need much better generals to survive what's coming.

---

[248] G.K. Chesterton, *The Everlasting Man* (1925) http://gutenberg.net.au/ebooks01/0100311.txt

APPENDIX
WHAT HAVE THE ROMANS EVER DONE FOR US?

A READING LIST

Chesterton held that aside from flowers at Easter and sausages at Christmas, "Everything else in the modern world is of Christian origin, even everything that seems most anti-Christian. The French Revolution is of Christian origin. The newspaper is of Christian origin. The anarchists are of Christian origin. Physical science is of Christian origin. The attack on Christianity is of Christian origin. There is one thing, and one thing only, in existence at the present day which can in any sense accurately be said to be of pagan origin, and that is Christianity."[249] As ever, he was right. The short answer to the question, "What good things about Western civilization came from the Church?" is: all of them.

It's beyond the scope of this book—it's beyond the scope of one hundred books—to give a full account of how indebted

---

[249] G.K. Chesterton, *Heretics* (1905) https://www.gutenberg.org/files/470/470-h/470-h.htm

we are to Christianity for everything we hold dear, but this chapter will provide some hints, and a short reading list, for those of you still not convinced that the Catholic Church is worth preserving, despite everything. Some of what follows will surprise you: decades of liberal indoctrination in college has planted dozens of ahistorical myths about the West in the popular consciousness, especially the intellectual debt we supposedly owe to Islam. Each of the examples I provide here gives a sense of the scope and depth and richness of the Western Christian tradition—and what we could lose if we say farewell to the Catholic Church. Indeed, what we're already losing as an enfeebled Church and an emasculated West slide into degenerate secularism and progressivism.

First of all, what we now know as "the West" is merely what was left over following the Muslim conquest of Christendom, which is why, according to historian Raymond Ibrahim, "Europe's self-identity never revolved around ethnicity or language…but rather religion. [Europe] was the last and most redoubtable bastion of Christendom to be conquered by Islam."[250] Hence the meme, popularized by yours truly, of "Reclaiming Constantinople."[251] In other words, Western identity is a product of Islamic aggression, defined by its Christianity. That's worth repeating: Christianity defines the West, and not race, geography, gender, or anything else the modern academy is preoccupied with. In what follows, I'll try to give as brief an account as possible of what makes the West so sensational and fabulous! And why we have God to thank for all of it.

---

[250] Raymond Ibrahim, *Sword and Scimitar: Fourteen Centuries of War Between Islam and the West* (New York: Da Capo Press, 2018), 9.

[251] https://www.breitbart.com/milo/2016/12/07/full-text-milo-msu-reclaiming-constantinople/

First off, our very idea of ourselves as distinct individuals is a product of Christianity. We are human beings, recognized as ensouled regardless of skin color, gender, or social class because we have a relationship with the Almighty and we are created in his image. Everything in the Western legal system depends on this definition of the individual as indivisible and uniquely worthy. It is the basis of equality before the law. Nothing in pagan, pre-medieval traditions speaks to equal status before God for all human beings regardless of ethnicity or sex, and Christianity does not recognize the "slave morality" of Nietzsche or Aristotle's belief that slavery was natural for some. Just as Christianity granted dignity to the lowest, it also humbled the mighty: King David was answerable to God for his sins, bound by the law just like everyone else. *Inventing the Individual: The Origins of Western Liberalism*[252] is a recent book on the subject.

Although the Bible accepts slavery as a fact of life—which, at the time, it was—slavery often ends in cultures that convert to Christianity, and in the Christian world it is Christians arguing with other Christians that brings an end to the practice. Slavery is still practiced throughout the world, especially in Islamic countries, but no longer exists in Christian nations. Only more religion can give us less modern slavery.[253] Rodney Stark, who has written many excellent and robust defenses of Christianity, specifically includes the end of slavery as one of the great accomplishments of

---

[252] Larry Siedentop, *Inventing the Individual: The Origins of Western Liberalism* (London: Allen Lane, 2014)
[253] http://news.trust.org/item/20180920131151-tbmj9/

Christianity in *For the Glory of God.*[254] Thomas Sowell makes a similar argument in *Black Rednecks and White Liberals.*[255]

A daft but persistent myth about Western civilization is that Christianity is bellicose. Modern secularists love to imagine that without the specter of "religion," life would be bliss, there would be no war, or death, or famine, and we'd all get to hold hands and dance in a circle around Stonehenge giving praise to life-giving Mother Gaia before tearing our clothes off and getting down to some pansexual opium orgy action. But real paganism was pretty bloody cruel, and Christians generally eschewed its worst excesses, such as gladiatorial combats. Christianity directly brought about the decline in violence that Steven Pinker wrongly attributes to the Enlightenment.[256] It did so as a response to the cruelty of paganism.

Moral barbarisms such as racism and the treatment of women and gays in the Islamic world are often reflexively described as "medieval." Actually, they're more like pre-medieval. The Middle Ages was characterized by a remarkable insensitivity to tribalism and race, thanks to the rise of Christianity. "Religion" is not a catch-all explanation for endemic violence—that's a left-wing myth. Only certain religions are, one of them in particular. The Crusades were considered acts of penance by knights; they weren't embarked upon for *houris.*

The Crusades were a defensive series of wars based not on skin color, but on religion. And to those who say, well,

---

[254] Rodney Stark, *For the Glory of God: How Monotheism Led to Reformations, Science, Witch-hunts, and the End of Slavery* (Princeton: Princeton University Press, 2013).

[255] Thomas Sowell, *Black Rednecks and White Liberals* (New York: Encounter Books, 2005).

[256] https://www.theguardian.com/books/2015/mar/13/john-gray-steven-pinker-wrong-violence-war-declining

can't we get rid of the religion to get rid of the wars? Nice try. History shows us that human beings would—and do—simply go to town on one another over something else. Isn't it better that we fight over the core values of our faith and civilization than over something as arbitrary as skin color? Isn't it more important to fight over culture than color? The Left has been trying to conflate "western" with "white" for decades, to scare conservatives off from defending their civilization too forcefully, lest they produce the dreaded, career-destroying allegation of racism.

Which is not to say that Christianity embraces or encourages violence. Unlike Islam, it doesn't. While Muslims are actively encouraged into holy war by their faith, Christians struggle endlessly to figure out how war is not inevitably sinful, as Raymond Ibrahim demonstrates in his new book *Sword and Scimitar*.[257] There's an enormous difference. For Augustine, a war was only just if it was declared by a legitimate authority—either a public authority or God—if it was defensive or fought to recover stolen possessions, if it was necessary, and if it was fought from a place of love. In the tenth and eleventh centuries, Christians further restricted the concept of just war by marking non-combatants as off-limits. What was appropriate in warfare, and all the noble traditions that eventually became the Geneva Convention and other similar international agreements about the proper conduct of war, emerge from this line of reasoning.

Most of what we cherish about the modern world in fact has its roots in the Middle Ages.[258] The Enlightenment, on the other hand, provided us with the scientific racism that fueled the Third Reich and the hubris that led to most of

---

[257] Raymond Ibrahim, *Sword and Scimitar* (Boston: Da Capo Press, 2018)
[258] http://theweek.com/articles/545429/did-enlightenment-cause-global-decline-violence

the modern world's unique horrors, such as the post-Christian awfulness of communism. David Bentley Hart's *Atheist Delusions*[259] provides a neat summary of the positive effects of Christianity on the old world. Islam, an inherently violent creed, was founded on *jihad*. Only Christianity has faced down paganism and won, and only Christianity truly preaches peace.

Speaking of things Steven Pinker gets wrong, we should debunk the left-wing myth that religion is at odds with science. Nope. Christianity grounds the study of the natural world in reason, as Benedict XVI's brilliant 2006 Regensburg lecture on "Faith, Reason, and the University" explained.[260] Benedict shows that it was Christianity, not Islam, that fostered scientific thinking, and that "the scientific ethos [is] the will to be obedient to the truth, and, as such, it embodies an attitude which belongs to the essential decisions of the Christian spirit." Early scientists wanted to explore the world around them and find out how it worked because it was a magnificent, and a mysterious, gift from God. For an account of how we ended up believing that science and religion were at loggerheads, check out Brad Gregory's *The Unintended Reformation: How A Religious Revolution Secularized Society*.[261] Or, for a less intimidating summary, my friend Rachel Fulton Brown at the University of Chicago has you covered. The needless schism between faith and reason has led us to an ugly place where our entire philosophical

---

[259] David Bentley Hart, *Atheist Delusions: The Christian Revolution and its Fashionable Enemies* (New Haven: Yale University Press, 2010).

[260] http://www.catholic-ew.org.uk/Home/News/2006/Full-Text-of-the-Pope-Benedict-XVI-s-Regensburg-Lecture

[261] Brad Gregory, *The Unintended Reformation: How a Religious Revolution Secularized Society* (Cambridge: Harvard University Press, 2012).

and political systems are rotting from within, absent their critical metaphysical undergirding.

We now live in a world in which there is no institutionally-accepted intellectual justification for our most profound moral and ethical beliefs, indeed no grounds on which to argue that we are anything other than meat-puppets driven by our most basic physical desires and needs. In Prof. Gregory's words: "Rights and dignity can be real only if human beings are more than biological matter." That is, only if human beings are in fact creatures made in the image and likeness of God—the theological basis of the claim for human dignity in the first place.

"But [to quote Prof. Gregory again] if nature is not creation [as our scientists are wont to argue], then there are no creatures, and human beings are just one more species that happened randomly to evolve, no more 'endowed by their creator with certain inalienable rights' than is any other bit of matter-energy. Then there simply are no rights, just as there are no persons, and no theorizing can conjure them into existence" [p. 381]. However much we may celebrate our hard-won liberties as individuals, if we have no Creator to endow us with rights, there are none. And, therefore, no basis whatsoever to restrain the state from rescinding them whenever it chooses.[262]

---

[262] https://fencingbearatprayer.blogspot.com/2012/05/reforming-reformation-review.html

One thing Christianity invented which modern life could do with more of is respect for women, as expressed in chivalry and consensual marriage. As Professor Fulton Brown argues, chivalry arose out of the desire to serve the Virgin Mary as the bride described in the Song of Songs, which deals specifically with sexual love.[263] Serving a woman civilizes and channels male aggression into protecting the weak while ennobling the woman who is the object of a man's affections. It also holds the woman to a particular set of standards, which is why unshaven, foul-mouthed feminists hate old-fashioned etiquette so much: both sexes have to make an effort, not just the man. Augustine wrote that he would never have recognized God's love, were it not for the love and prayerfulness of his mother, Monica. But he was not under the modern delusion that men and women are just the same, absent a few "social constructs."

The Church invented consensual marriage by insisting that the woman also say, "I do." This strengthened a woman's position as sacramental equal to her husband, as George Duby's classic account, *The Knight, the Lady and the Priest: The Making of Modern Marriage in Medieval France*,[264] explains. As the writer Michael Walsh puts it, "Christianity transformed women from chattel and helpless rape victims into human beings (a trick of cultural prestidigitation that Islam has not managed to accomplish in well over a millennium) who may not have had the political rights of men but who had the human rights of men…. Where Christianity,

---

[263] Rachel Fulton Brown, *Mary and the Art of Prayer: The Hours of the Virgin in Medieval Christian Life and Thought* (New York: Columbia University Press, 2017), chapter 5.

[264] Georges Duby, *The Knight, the Lady, and the Priest: The Making of Modern Marriage in Medieval France,* trans. Barbara Bray (Chicago: The University of Chicago Press, 1983).

through its liberation of women, forces men to improve themselves morally, imparting the virtue of self-restraint, Islam seeks to protect the weaker sex—men—from the stronger, and so allows them to beat and even murder the females in their orbits."[265] Anthony Esolen has written that Christians insisted on co-ed baptisms, because all were one under God and that Jesus was seen first at Easter by women, before his apostles. Romans cherished and revered their wives and shunned sexual practices that put them and their spouses at risk.

The oracle at Delphi said, "Know thyself." But it was Christian monks reciting the psalms who made self-examination and confession a spiritual discipline. Recitation of the psalms was intended to produce the same emotions as the psalmist, especially those of contrition. Augustine of Hippo's *Confessions* is the best-known example in literature of someone wrestling about his life of sin before conversion. Medieval Christians were even trained to examine themselves for sins, not only sexual but those of the soul, too. Ignatius Loyola examined his conscience long before Freud made a science of self-reflection.

It's not just psychoanalysis—many of Christianity's woes find their etiology in its own virtues: its embrace and elevation of the feminine has become an emasculated clerisy, its social justice metastasized into modern progressivism, and the idea that one culture might recognize the value in another has become an unthinking modern obsession with multiculturalism. In AD 601, Pope Gregory the Great told Abbot Mellitus not to destroy the pagan temples he found in Anglo-Saxon England, and instead consecrate them and adapt them for Christian worship. Bartolomé de las Casas

---

[265] Michael Walsh, *The Fiery Angel: Art, Culture, Sex, Politics and the Struggle for the Soul of the West* (New York: Encounter Books, 2018), 77.

argued that the Aztecs were acting from reason when they sacrificed humans to their gods, and that they were civilized and rational in offering the most precious thing they could to their deities. Their only failing was lacking the truth of revelation about what kind of offering would most please God.[266] He suggested they should be taught Christianity, rather than murdered for making mistakes.

Christians have bent over backwards to understand other cultures and welcome them into the faith, rather than cleansing the earth of any trace of prior religions, as Islamic fanatics regularly do, because the latter follow a totalitarian belief system that cannot tolerate the existence of outside authority. The root of this multicultural appreciation is, of course, Pentecost, when the people gathered in Jerusalem for a feast to hear the apostles speaking in their own tongues.[267] Like capitalism, Christianity has been resilient and adaptable, because it values labor and creativity. George Gilder's *Wealth and Poverty*[268] explains how the free market depends upon openness to the divine.

Dorothy Sayers' *Mind of the Maker*[269] reminds us that the central metaphor of Christianity is of God as a maker, as one who labored to create the world, which Tolkien understood as a writer and explored in his *Mythopoeia*.[270] Because we are made in the image and likeness of a maker, we too are called upon to make art. That's not to say Christianity wants everyone to be a perfumed aesthete: physical labor is not looked down on by Christians as it is by Western elites today. Like

---

[266] Bartolomé de las Casas, *In Defense of the Indians*, trans. Stafford Poole (DeKalb: Northern Illinois University Press, 1992).

[267] Acts 2

[268] George Gilder, *Wealth and Poverty* (Washington, DC: Regnery, 2012)

[269] Dorothy Sayers, *The Mind of the Maker* (New York: Harcourt Brace, 1941).

[270] http://vrici.lojban.org/~cowan/mythopoeia.html

this author, Jesus spent his days working with wood. And Peter was a fisherman, which is about the most smelly and disgusting job around.

Christianity has provided infinitely more pleasure than poison, especially when it comes to music and the written word. It's an easier sell to people that art and music are compatible with faith, since people have such similarly uplifting experiences of both. But, again, we must turn to Benedict for the full picture. His 2008 lecture to the Collège[271] des Bernadins, "Meeting with Representatives from the World of Culture," shows how music depends on faith to succeed. Michael Walsh's *The Fiery Angel: Art, Culture, Sex, Politics and the Struggle for the Soul of the West* is a recent addition to the literature. It only glances at the medieval but does explain how late medieval polyphony trained the West to think in multiple voices and work towards an aesthetic experience that was "satisfying both emotionally and formally," uniting the passions and reason together. Islam has no such musical tradition, and therefore lacks an awareness of temporality and the satisfaction of understanding emerging from storytelling. Aside from one truly noteworthy moment of sexual passion I enjoyed in late 2017, stepping inside St. Peter's Basilica in Rome was the most spiritually uplifting and remarkable experience of my life. Please, make sure you do it at least once before you die, to understand how art, architecture, music, and literature fuse together in celebration of God and are indivisible from His creation.

Novelists in the eighteenth and nineteenth centuries were masters at deploying quotidian details from daily life, reflecting how Christianity so often works: from the mundane to the transcendent. Augustine's ideal of God speaking

---

[271] http://w2.vatican.va/content/benedict-xvi/en/speeches/2008/september/documents/hf_ben-xvi_spe_20080912_parigi-cultura.html

in the humble style we call *sermo humilis*. Christian authors often address the simple and everyday as a way of lifting the mind to understanding. The use of the imagination for the sake of empathy is an invention of Christian art, designed to recall Christ's humanity and to help us empathize with his suffering on the cross. This is the heart of medieval devotion. The effect of empathy on art was to elevate ordinary people into proper subjects for artistic exploration and give them status as protagonists, an early example of which is Chaucer's *Canterbury Tales*, with its story-telling pilgrims from all walks of life. While the ancients had a rhetorical practice of taking on different characters, Christianity added the desire to *feel* on behalf of another, which was the innovation that made the majority of literature possible.[272]

The Canterbury Tales is one of the earliest examples in the English language of genuinely funny writing, the sort of thing you might guffaw at in the library by accident—especially the more profane passages in the Miller's Tale, which have provided literature students joy for generations.[273] And it's joy that Chesterton correctly identifies as *the* pre-eminently unique characteristic of Christianity. He is, as ever, worth quoting at length:

> Joy, which was the small publicity of the pagan, is the gigantic secret of the Christian. And as I close this chaotic volume I open again the strange small book from which all Christianity came; and I am again haunted by a kind of confirmation. The tremendous figure which fills the Gospels towers in this respect,

[272] Rachel Fulton Brown, *From Judgment to Passion: Devotion to Christ and the Virgin Mary, 800–1200* (New York: Columbia University Press, 2002).
[273] http://bettermyths.com/the-miller-is-one-drunk-motherfucker/

as in every other, above all the thinkers who
ever thought themselves tall. His pathos was
natural, almost casual. The Stoics, ancient and
modern, were proud of concealing their tears.
He never concealed His tears; He showed them
plainly on His open face at any daily sight, such
as the far sight of His native city. Yet He concealed something. Solemn supermen and imperial diplomatists are proud of restraining their
anger. He never restrained His anger. He flung
furniture down the front steps of the Temple,
and asked men how they expected to escape the
damnation of Hell. Yet He restrained something. I say it with reverence; there was in that
shattering personality a thread that must be
called shyness. There was something that He
hid from all men when He went up a moun-
tain to pray. There was something that He covered constantly by abrupt silence or impetuous
isolation. There was some one thing that was
too great for God to show us when He walked
upon our earth; and I have sometimes fancied
that it was His mirth.[274]

Elsewhere in his *Heretics*, Chesterton characterizes the
joyful, unreasonable virtues that are Christian innovations—
faith, hope, and charity—with their pagan antecedents:

The real difference between Paganism and
Christianity is perfectly summed up in the difference between the pagan, or natural, virtues,

---

[274] G.K. Chesterton, *Orthodoxy* (1908) http://www.gutenberg.org/
ebooks/16769

and those three virtues of Christianity which the Church of Rome calls virtues of grace. The pagan, or rational, virtues are such things as justice and temperance, and Christianity has adopted them. The three mystical virtues which Christianity has not adopted, but invented, are faith, hope, and charity.

Now much easy and foolish Christian rhetoric could easily be poured out upon those three words, but I desire to confine myself to the two facts which are evident about them. The first evident fact (in marked contrast to the delusion of the dancing pagan)—the first evident fact, I say, is that the pagan virtues, such as justice and temperance, are the sad virtues, and that the mystical virtues of faith, hope, and charity are the gay and exuberant virtues. And the second evident fact, which is even more evident, is the fact that the pagan virtues are the reasonable virtues, and that the Christian virtues of faith, hope, and charity are in their essence as unreasonable as they can be.[275]

J.R.R. Tolkien wrote, in letter 310 to Camilla Unwin, that the purpose of life was to praise the Creator with hymns of joy.[276] Laughter underpins the divine comedy of Christianity. Catholic Christians—medieval ones, at least—are always about to burst into laughter or song. Their Churches are

---

[275] G.K. Chesterton, *Heretics* (1905) https://www.gutenberg.org/files/470/470-h/470-h.htm

[276] Letter 310 To Camilla Unwin, 20 May 1969, in *The Letters of J.R.R. Tolkien,* ed. Humphrey Carpenter with Christopher Tolkien (London: George Allen & Unwin, 1981).

adorned with mischievous, sexually explicit carvings.[277] Christianity is never solemn for long, and never in the way Islam and paganism are. My personal motto, laughter and war, borrowed from Chesterton, is rooted in this fact: that Christianity's greatest gift to us is joy, and that, without God, laughter is hollow—and fleeting.

---

[277] https://elpais.com/elpais/2018/07/31/inenglish/1533051824_344537. html

ACKNOWLEDGMENTS

In the mysterious communion of saints, observes Flannery O'Connor, there are "lines that join the most diverse lives, and that hold us fast in Christ." I am indebted to the many conservative and Christian writers and scholars whose reporting and punditry provided such good raw material for this book. Now, finally, they know how enthusiastically I am bringing up the rear. So, my thanks to Lee Podles, who was very generous with his time, Anthony Esolen, David French, Matthew Schmitz, Ross Douthat, Edward Pentin, Rodney Stark, Michael Brendan Dougherty, Sohrab Ahmari, Rod Dreher, and others.

I try not to hurt my friends and acquaintances, so I usually do not associate myself with them publicly. However, Professor Rachel Fulton Brown of the University of Chicago offered many helpful suggestions, as did Scott Walter and Prof. Mark Bauerlein, and it would be wrong not to thank them. Chadwick Moore tells me when I've used a joke too often, or it's not as funny as I think it is, which happens often. And I am grateful to David Bernstein at Bombardier for taking me on—fitting, since his imprint was founded because of me. Catholicism certainly makes for strange bedfellows. But then the Lord we worship never shunned whores, adulterers, or even tax collectors.

INDEX

ABOUT THE AUTHOR

Milo Yiannopoulos is an award-winning journalist, a *New York Times* bestselling author, an international political celebrity, a free speech martyr, an accomplished entrepreneur, a Louis Vuitton addict, a Mariah Carey superfan, a hair icon, a penitent and, to the annoyance of his many enemies, an exceedingly happy person. He is one of the most sought-after speakers in the world, invited by foreign governments, wealthy individuals and even the occasional courageous private company to share his unique blend of laughter and war. Milo lurches from improbable success to improbable success, loathed by the Left and establishment Republicans alike. His first book, *Dangerous*, sold over 200,000 copies, despite never being reviewed in any major publication. Milo lives in Florida with his husband, John.

Made in the USA
Monee, IL
06 November 2019